Down a Dark Street

An anthology of American crime stories

selected by

C. E. J. Smith

Edward Arnold

First published 1973
by Edward Arnold (Publishers) Ltd,
25 Hill Street,
London W1X 8LL

ISBN: 0 7131 1808 3

Set in 11 on 12 point Caledonia
and printed in Great Britain by
William Clowes & Sons, Limited
London, Beccles and Colchester

Contents

Preface

In his essay *The Simple Art of Murder* Raymond Chandler refers to '. . . the flustered old ladies – of both sexes (or no sex) and almost all ages – who like their murders scented with magnolia blossoms and do not care to be reminded that murder is an act of infinite cruelty. . . .'

In an interview with Marcelle Bernstein, printed in an article in the *Observer*, Agatha Christie is quoted as saying: 'I don't like messy deaths. Anyway, I'm more interested in peaceful people who die in their beds and no one knows why. I don't like violence. I once collected papers for three weeks and every day there was somebody murdered, some girl killed, some child missing and strangled. I think it's a sign of the times.'

When I looked through the collections of detective stories available for school use I was struck by the all-pervasive scent of magnolia. It appeared that crime – particularly lethal crime – was the playground of elegant young aristocrats, jolly spinster ladies, and eccentric adventurers. Methods of murder required the scientific knowledge of an Oxbridge don, the stop-watch precision of a Three A's timekeeper, and the nerves of a high-wire walker, whereas the motives were those of a spoilt child of ten. I was forced to agree with Michael Marland's stricture: '. . . empty elegance of language in the service of pointless ingenuity of plot'.

The purpose of this anthology is to make equally available examples of another style of crime writing. This 'tough' school of writing began with Dashiell Hammett, an ex-Pinkerton detective who wrote for the American pulp magazine *Black Mask*. It had off-shoots in the work of Ernest Hemingway and William Faulkner, and it reached its height as a medium for the crime story in the books of Raymond Chandler. Today, its finest exponent is Ross Macdonald.

It is a type of writing that has often been denigrated. Of Chandler's first novel a reviewer wrote: 'Lots of nastily addled ten-minute eggs rampaging in tough but high-gloss lingo from super-heated start to fantastic finish.' It is a type of writing that has suffered from its imitators. From the harsh realism of Hammett, the detailed accuracy of Hemingway, and the cool subtleties of Chandler we have descended to the violent excesses of Spillane and the banalities of Jansen.

There is an unfortunate tendency to classify all writing of this type under the heading 'American hard-boiled' and dismiss it. But it has been too influential a *genre* and attracted the attention of too many thoughtful critics to be pushed to one side so easily.

As Chandler said of him: 'Hammett gave murder back to the kind of people who commit it for reasons, not just to provide a corpse; and with the means at hand, not with hand-wrought duelling pistols, curare, and tropical fish. He put these people down on paper as they are, and he made them talk and think in the language they customarily used for these purposes.'

In *Imaginary Interviews* André Gide wrote: 'Dashiell Hammett's dialogues, in which every character is trying to deceive all the others and in which the truth slowly becomes visible through the haze of deception can be compared only with the best of Hemingway.'

Somerset Maugham writing of 'The Decline and Fall of the Detective Story' voiced the opinion :'To my mind the two best novelists of the hard-boiled school are Dashiell Hammett and Raymond Chandler . . . (they) have created characters that we can believe in. They are only a little more heightened, a little more vivid, than people we have all come across.'

This emphasis on character rather than complexity of plot was stressed by the editor of *Black Mask*, Joseph T. Shaw: 'We wanted simplicity for the sake of clarity, plausibility and belief. We wanted action, but we held that action is meaningless unless it involves recognizable human character in three-dimensional form.' Anthony Boucher, *New York Times* critic, believed: 'The pulps brought pace and vigour and physical and emotional impact to the detective story: they made it approach the crude realities of American police work and the daily routine of the private operative.'

These then are the qualities of the American crime story. There are constant reminders that crime is a nasty, brutal business, carried out by vicious people in mean streets for selfish motives.

In this collection it is the work of the 'serious' writer, Ernest Hemingway, that is most violent. Even the humorist, Damon Runyon, who created his own small world of 'guys and dolls' in his own distinctive prose style, cannot disguise what E. C. Bentley called the 'violence, and dissipation, and predatory worthlessness' of his characters. William Faulkner and Arthur Miller each produce stories to show that the same evil forces are at work whether the setting is inhospitable hill country or affluent suburbia. Stanley Ellin has given his starting point as: 'a sociological concept: the tragedy of the civil-service mentality which sells everything for economic security; the effects of a murder on an apparently rock-ribbed middle-class family; the veering of American youth to mink-coat-and-Cadillac standards'. Donald E. Westlake and Joe Gores have transferred the violence from the incidents to the emotions. Only in a very early story from a very young F. Scott Fitzgerald does the faint perfume of magnolia creep in, with the trains and carriages, and a Chief of Police who needs to buy a fresh brace of revolvers.

The last word can be left with Raymond Chandler in a further paragraph from his *Simple Art of Murder*: 'The realist in murder writes of a world in which gangsters can rule nations and almost rule cities, in which hotels and apartment houses and celebrated restaurants are owned by men who made their money out of brothels, . . . where no man can walk down a dark street in safety because law and order are things we talk about but refrain from practising; a world where you may witness a hold-up in broad daylight and see who did it, but you will fade quickly back into the crowd rather than tell anyone, because the hold-up men may have friends with long guns. . . . It is not a very fragrant world, but it is the world you live in, and certain writers with tough minds and a cool spirit of detachment can make very interesting and even amusing patterns out of it.'

CEJS
Icknield County Secondary School
Wantage

Notes on the authors

RAYMOND CHANDLER

'Chandler had a fine feeling for the sound and value of words, and he added to it a very sharp eye for places, things, people, and the wisecracks (*this out-of-date word seems still the right one*) *that in their tone and timing are almost perfect.'*

Julian Symons, *Bloody Murder*

'He is not just one more detective writer – he is a craftsman so brilliant, he has an imagination so wholly original that no consideration of modern American literature ought, I think, to exclude him.'

Elizabeth Bowen in *The Tatler*

Raymond Chandler was born in Chicago on July 23rd 1888. At the age of eight he was brought to England by his Irish Quaker mother. He was educated at Dulwich College where he excelled in classics. After completing his education in France and Germany he became a free-lance journalist and contributed reviews, paragraphs and essays to *The Westminster Gazette* and *The Spectator*. In 1912 he returned to the U.S.A. and on the outbreak of World War I enlisted with the Canadian Gordon Highlanders. After service in France he returned to California and worked as an accountant before becoming an executive with five independent oil companies. During the depression he lost his job and while 'wandering up and down the Pacific Coast in an automobile' began reading pulp fiction. He decided to try his hand at this and his first story was published in *Black Mask* in 1933. His first novel followed in 1939 and during the next twenty years he became the accepted master of the crime story. He died in 1959.

STANLEY ELLIN

'... *Mr Ellin's talent grew and matured and became a thing of beauty ... with the years, with his unflagging zest, his almost incredible conscientiousness, his hypersensitivity to the impact of horror which lurks not only in the 'specialities' of life but equally, perhaps even more shockingly, in the 'orderly world' about us—with and through all these Stanley Ellin's stature as a writer grew and his work flashed new tones; for undeniably there are bigger meanings in his later stories, larger problems delved into, subtler nuances revealed in his characters and in the events that lead to – and inevitably follow – the tragedies of modern living.*'

Ellery Queen, Foreword to *Mystery Stories*, 1956

Stanley Ellin was born in New York City on 6th October 1916. In 1936 he graduated B.A. from Brooklyn College. He worked for a newspaper and then turned to writing radio scripts. Before becoming a full-time writer he worked as a farmer, a teacher and a steel worker. During the Second World War he served in the U.S. Army. In his spare time he wrote the first draft of a short story, 'The Speciality of the House' which won a Special Prize from the Ellery Queen Mystery Magazine. Further short stories were equally successful and in 1958 a collection called *Mystery Stories* was selected as one of the 100 most important books of the year. Later the same collection was included in the *Sunday Times* List of A Hundred Great Mystery Collections. Mr Ellin has won the 'Edgar' Award of the Mystery Writers of America three times.

He is married and has one daughter. Julian Symons has described him as 'plump and amiable a little awkward, rather like a medium-sized friendly bear'.

WILLIAM FAULKNER

William Faulkner was born on 25th September 1897. He grew up in Oxford, Mississippi where he received a 'desultory education'. He began work in his grandfather's bank but left Oxford for Toronto in 1918 to enter flight training in Britain's Royal Air Force. He became an honorary second lieutenant after the armistice. In 1919 he registered in the University of Mississippi and wrote some stories for the University paper. He had many jobs – shop assistant in a bookstore, temporary postmaster, freelance journalist in New Orleans, rum runner, barnstormer, golfer, lumber mill worker, carpenter and painter – before he evolved his own style of writing and began his novels. In 1931 he wrote *Sanctuary*, deliberately making it as horrifying as possible. This brought his name before the public and soon he was lured to Hollywood where he worked off and on for more than twenty years. He was awarded the Nobel Prize in 1949. After a lifetime of writing he died in 1962, generally acknowledged as a great American novelist.

F. SCOTT FITZGERALD

F. Scott Fitzgerald was born in St Paul, Minnesota on 24th September 1896. He was educated at St Paul Academy and the Newman School, New Jersey. Before serving in the First World War as an infantry lieutenant he studied at Princeton. After demobilization he went to New York to find work on the newspapers. After he had been rejected by seven editors he took a job writing advertising slogans. Meanwhile he was writing short stories and when one or two were accepted he returned to St Paul to work on a novel, *This Side of Paradise*. This brought him great success as the voice of his generation. He continued to write, and married Zelda Sayre, another writer. They lived in Paris, New York, Long Island and on the Riviera, pursuing an existence that led eventually to Zelda's incurable mental illness and Fitzgerald's nervous breakdown. He suffered great emotional and financial strain and at the age of 44 died of a heart attack in Hollywood where he was working as what he himself called a 'literary hack'.

JOE GORES

There appear to be very few biographical details available for Mr Gores. His short stories featuring the operatives of the Daniel Kearny agency which specialize in frauds, defalcations, and embezzlements began to appear in *Ellery Queen's Mystery Magazine* in 1967. A novel, *The Predators,* was published here by the New English Library. He writes a hard, contemporary story in a hard, contemporary style.

DASHIELL HAMMETT

'He was spare, frugal, hard-boiled, but he did over and over again what only the best writers can ever do at all. He wrote scenes that seemed never to have been written before.'

Raymond Chandler in *The Simple Art of Murder*

'. . . his greatest service to the crime story was . . . that he took it by the scruff of the neck and put it where it really belonged. After Hammett crime came out of the library and into reality. . . .'

John Welcome in the introduction to *Best Crime Stories*

Dashiell Hammett was born in St Mary's County, Maryland on 27th May 1894. He grew up in Philadelphia and Baltimore, attending the Baltimore Polytechnic Institute. He left school at fourteen and, after working as newsboy, labourer, timekeeper, machine-operator and stevedore, he became an operative for the Pinkerton Detective agency. He was connected with the Fatty Arbuckle case, and was promoted for his part in catching a man who stole a Ferris wheel. While serving as a sergeant with the Motor Ambulance Corps during the First World War he contracted tuberculosis. He attempted to resume his work as a detective but was forced to give up. He turned to writing, and using his previous experience soon became one of the most highly-praised and influential authors in the detective genre. His finest story is *The Maltese Falcon.* He worked at night and sometimes continued for 36 hours at a sitting. Most of the later part of his life was spent in Hollywood. In World War II he enlisted as a private and served overseas. In 1951 he was jailed for refusing to reveal the source of bail funds of the Civil Rights Congress. He died in 1961.

ERNEST HEMINGWAY

'. . . you picked out the sharp details from life that had aroused your own emotion and, if you described them accurately, in their proper sequence and without closing your eyes to violence and horror, you had something that would continue to arouse the emotion of your readers.'

Ernest Hemingway, *Death in the Afternoon*

'He is one of those who, honestly and undauntedly, reproduces the genuine features of the hard countenance of the age.'

Nobel Prize Citation

Ernest Hemingway was born in Illinois in 1898. While still at school he made many hunting and fishing trips to North Michigan. At fifteen he ran away from home. After graduating from Oak Park High School he took a job on the *Kansas City Star.* Later he went to Europe as a volunteer ambulance driver in France. He was wounded on the Italian Front. After the war he went to the Middle East as correspondent for the *Toronto Star.* Then he settled in Paris and began his work as a writer. Over the years he produced many short stories and a number of novels which established his reputation as a stylist and a master of dialogue. He was intensely interested in bull-fighting, big-game-hunting, and deep-sea fishing. He was a war correspondent in Spain during the Civil War and in other parts of Europe during the Second World War. In 1954 he was awarded the Nobel Prize for Literature. He died in 1961.

ARTHUR MILLER

Arthur Miller was born on the 17th October 1915. After 'uninspired schooldays' at high school, during which he rose early to deliver bread for a local bakery, he took a job in an automobile parts warehouse to work his way through college. While at the University of Michigan, from which he graduated in 1938, he worked as night editor on the *Michigan Daily.* He seems to have had that variety of work that is so often an American author's background: truckdriver, waiter, crewman on a tanker, shipfitter, factory worker, helper in the Brooklyn Navy Yard. He wrote radio plays and also for the theatre. *All My Sons* was produced in 1947, and in 1949 *Death of a Salesman* won a Pulitzer Prize. He clashed with the Congressional Un-American Activities Committee. In 1956 he married Marilyn Monroe and later wrote the script for *The Misfits*, her last film.

DAMON RUNYON

'He broke into literature, quite suddenly, with a hilarious short story of the gangsters and crooks infesting a certain section of Broadway . . . He followed it up with many others of the same sort . . . told in a tone and a language that make up one of the richest contributions to comic literature in our time.'

E. C. Bentley in the introduction to *Runyon on Broadway*

Damon Runyon was born in Manhattan, Kansas in 1884. At 17 he volunteered to fight in the Philippines. After bluffing his way into the Army he was wounded twice. He returned home in 1900 and became a freelance journalist. In 1907 he joined the staff of *The Denver Post.* He wrote on politics, sport, crime and anything else that offered. In 1911 he became a sports writer for *The New York American* and earned a nationwide reputation as a reporter. In the First World War he fought in Germany. After his return his marriage collapsed as he spent most of his time enjoying the night-life he was to write about. In 1932 he published *Guys and Dolls*, stories about the gangsters and crooks to be seen on the pavements on Broadway. His unique style and range of emotion earned him great popularity, and many of the stories were filmed. Damon Runyon died in New York on 10th December 1946.

DONALD E. WESTLAKE

Donald Westlake was born in Brooklyn, New York in 1934. He grew up and attended school in Albany. During his years at Chaplain and Harpur Colleges he edited the college newspapers. He served in Germany with the American Air Force, has worked as an actor, and during 1958–1959 was editor in a literary agency. In 1960 his first novel *The Mercenaries* won an award from the Mystery Writers of America. Since then he has written over thirty crime novels, many under his own name and many as Richard Stark. Mr Westlake, who was described by his publisher as 'an unnasty-looking man with a talent for writing some of the nastiest tales to come out of America since the end of the War', is married and has four sons.

The Gatewood Caper

Dashiell Hammett

Harvey Gatewood had issued orders that I was to be admitted as soon as I arrived, so it took me only a little less than fifteen minutes to thread my way past the door-keepers, office boys, and secretaries who filled up most of the space between the Gatewood Lumber Corporation's front door and the president's private office. His office was large, all mahogany and bronze and green plush, with a mahogany desk as big as a bed in the centre of the floor.

Gatewood, leaning across the desk, began to bark at me as soon as the obsequious clerk who had bowed me in bowed himself out.

'My daughter was kidnapped last night! I want the gang that did it if it takes every cent I got!'

'Tell me about it,' I suggested.

But he wanted results, it seemed, and not questions, and so I wasted nearly an hour getting information that he could have given me in fifteen minutes.

He was a big bruiser of a man, something over 200 pounds of hard red flesh, and a czar from the top of his bullet head to the toes of his shoes that would have been at least number twelves if they hadn't been made to measure.

He had made his several millions by sandbagging everybody that stood in his way, and the rage he was burning up with now didn't make him any easier to deal with.

His wicked jaw was sticking out like a knob of granite and his eyes were filmed with blood – he was in a lovely frame of mind. For a while it looked as if the Continental Detective Agency was going to lose a client, because I'd made up my mind that he was going to tell me all I wanted to know, or I'd chuck the job.

But finally I got the story out of him.

His daughter Audrey had left their house on Clay Street at about 7 o'clock the preceding evening, telling her maid that she was going for a walk. She had not returned that night – though Gatewood had not known that until after he had read the letter that came this morning.

The letter had been from someone who said that she had been kidnapped. It demanded $50,000 for her release, and instructed Gatewood to get the money ready in hundred-dollar bills – so that there would be no delay when he was told the manner in which the money was to be paid over to his daughter's captors. As proof that the demand was not a hoax, a lock of the girl's hair, a ring she always wore, and a brief note from her, asking her father to comply with the demands, had been enclosed.

Gatewood had received the letter at his office and had telephoned to his house immediately. He had been told that the girl's bed had not been slept in the previous night and that none of the servants had seen her since she started out for her walk. He had then notified the police, turning the letter over to them, and a few minutes later he had decided to employ private detectives also.

'Now,' he burst out, after I had wormed these things out of him, and he had told me that he knew nothing of his daughter's associates or habits, 'go ahead and do something! I'm not paying you to sit around and talk about it!'

'What are you going to do?' I asked.

'Me? I'm going to put those — behind bars if it takes every cent I've got in the world!'

'Sure! But first you get that $50,000 ready, so you can give it to them when they ask for it.'

He clicked his jaw shut and thrust his face into mine.

'I've never been clubbed into doing anything in my life! And I'm too old to start now!' he said. 'I'm going to call these people's bluff!'

'That's going to make it lovely for your daughter. But,

aside from what it'll do to her, it's the wrong play. Fifty thousand isn't a whole lot to you, and paying it over will give us two chances that we haven't got now. One when the payment is made – a chance either to nab whoever comes for it or get a line on them. And the other when your daughter is returned. No matter how careful they are, it's a cinch she'll be able to tell us something that will help us grab them.'

He shook his head angrily, and I was tired of arguing with him. So I left, hoping he'd see the wisdom of the course I had advised before it was too late.

At the Gatewood residence I found butlers, second men, chauffeurs, cooks, maids, upstairs girls, downstairs girls, and a raft of miscellaneous flunkies – he had enough servants to run a hotel.

What they told me amounted to this: the girl had not received a phone call, note by messenger or telegram – the time-honoured devices for luring a victim out to a murder or abduction – before she left the house. She had told her maid that she would be back within an hour or two; but the maid had not been alarmed when her mistress failed to return all that night.

Audrey was the only child, and since her mother's death she had come and gone to suit herself. She and her father didn't hit it off very well together – their natures were too much alike, I gathered – and he never knew where she was. There was nothing unusual about her remaining away all night. She seldom bothered to leave word when she was going to stay overnight with friends.

She was nineteen years old, but looked several years older, about five feet five inches tall, and slender. She had blue eyes, brown hair – very thick and long – was pale and very nervous. Her photographs, of which I took a handful, showed that her eyes were large, her nose small and regular and her chin pointed.

She was not beautiful, but in the one photograph where a smile had wiped off the sullenness of her mouth, she was at least pretty.

When she left the house she was wearing a light tweed skirt and jacket with a London tailor's label in them, a buff silk shirtwaist with stripes a shade darker, brown wool stockings, low-heeled brown oxfords, and an untrimmed gray felt hat.

I went up to her rooms – she had three on the third floor – and looked through all her stuff. I found nearly a bushel of photographs of men, boys, and girls; and a great stack of letters of varying degrees of intimacy, signed with a wide assortment of names and nicknames. I made notes of all the addresses I found.

Nothing in her rooms seemed to have any bearing on her abduction, but there was a chance that one of the names and addresses might be of someone who had served as a decoy. Also, some of her friends might be able to tell us something of value.

I dropped in at the Agency and distributed the names and addresses among the three operatives who were idle, sending them out to see what they could dig up.

Then I reached the police detectives who were working on the case – O'Gar and Thode – by telephone, and went down to the Hall of Justice to meet them. Lusk, a post office inspector, was also there. We turned the job around and around, looking at it from every angle, but not getting very far. We were all agreed, however, that we couldn't take a chance on any publicity, or work in the open, until the girl was safe.

They had had a worse time with Gatewood than I – he had wanted to put the whole thing in the newspapers, with the offer of a reward, photographs and all. Of course, Gatewood was right in claiming that this was the most effective way of catching the kidnappers – but it would have been tough on his daughter if her captors happened to be persons of sufficiently hardened character. And kidnappers as a rule aren't lambs.

I looked at the letter they had sent. It was printed with pencil on ruled paper of the kind that is sold in pads by every stationery dealer in the world. The envelope was just as common, also addressed in pencil, and postmarked *San Francisco, September 20, 9 p.m.* That was the night she had been seized.

The letter read:

> Sir:
>
> We have your charming daughter and place a value of $50,000 upon her. You will get the money

ready in $100 bills at once so there will be no delay when we tell you how it is to be paid over to us.

We beg to assure you that things will go badly with your daughter should you not do as you are told, or should you bring the police into this matter, or should you do anything foolish.

$50,000 is only a small fraction of what you stole while we were living in mud and blood in France for you, and we mean to get that much or else!

Three.

A peculiar note in several ways. They are usually written with a great pretence of partial illiterateness. Almost always there's an attempt to lead suspicion astray. Perhaps the ex-service stuff was there for that purpose – or perhaps not.

Then there was a postscript:

We know someone who will buy her even after we are through with her – in case you won't listen to reason.

The letter from the girl was written jerkily on the same kind of paper, apparently with the same pencil.

Daddy –

Please do as they ask! I am so afraid –

Audrey

A door at the other end of the room opened, and a head came through.

'O'Gar! Thode! Gatewood just called up. Get up to his office right away!'

The four of us tumbled out of the Hall of Justice and into a police car.

Gatewood was pacing his office like a maniac when we pushed aside enough hirelings to get to him. His face was hot with blood and his eyes had an insane glare in them.

'She just phoned me!' he cried thickly, when he saw us.

It took a minute or two to get him calm enough to tell us about it.

'She called me on the phone. Said "Oh, Daddy! Do something! I can't stand this – they're killing me!" I asked her if she knew where she was, and she said, "No, but I can see Twin Peaks from here. There's three men and a woman, and –" And then I heard a man curse, and a sound as if he had struck her, and the phone went dead. I tried to get central to give me the number, but she couldn't! It's a damned outrage the way the telephone system is run. We pay enough for service. God knows, and we . . .'

O'Gar scratched his head and turned away from Gatewood. 'In sight of Twin Peaks! There are hundreds of houses that are!'

Gatewood meanwhile had finished denouncing the telephone company and was pounding on his desk with a paperweight to attract our attention.

'Have you people done anything at all?' he demanded.

I answered him with another question: 'Have you got the money ready?'

'No,' he said, 'I won't be held up by anybody!'

But he said it mechanically, without his usual conviction – the talk with his daughter had shaken him out of some of his stubbornness. He was thinking of her safety a little now instead of only his own fighting spirit.

We went at him hammer and tongs for a few minutes, and after a while he sent a clerk out for the money.

We split up the field then. Thode was to take some men from headquarters and see what he could find in the Twin Peaks end of town; but we weren't very optimistic over the prospects there – the territory was too large.

Lusk and O'Gar were to carefully mark the bills that the clerk brought from the bank, and then stick as close to Gatewood as they could without attracting attention. I was to go out to Gatewood's house and stay there.

The abductors had plainly instructed Gatewood to get the money ready immediately so that they could arrange to get it on short notice – not giving him time to communicate with anyone or make plans.

Gatewood was to get hold of the newspapers, give them the whole story, with the $10,000 reward he was offering for the abductor's capture, to be published as soon as the girl was safe – so we would get the help of publicity at the earliest possible moment without jeopardizing the girl.

The police in all the neighbouring towns had already been notified – that had been done before the girl's phone message had assured us that she was held in San Francisco.

Nothing happened at the Gatewood residence all that evening. Harvey Gatewood came home early; and after dinner he paced his library floor and drank whisky until bedtime, demanding every few minutes that we, the detectives in the case, do something besides sit around like a lot of damned mummies. O'Gar, Lusk, and Thode were out in the street, keeping an eye on the house and neighbourhood.

At midnight Harvey Gatewood went to bed. I declined a bed in favour of the library couch, which I dragged over beside the telephone, an extension of which was in Gatewood's bedroom.

At 2.30 the telephone bell rang. I listened in while Gatewood talked from his bed.

A man's voice, crisp and curt: 'Gatewood?'

'Yes.'

'Got the dough?'

'Yes.'

Gatewood's voice was thick and blurred – I could imagine the boiling that was going on inside him.

'Good!' came the brisk voice. 'Put a piece of paper around it and leave the house with it, right away! Walk down Clay Street, keeping on the same side as your house. Don't walk too fast and keep walking. If everything's all right, and there's no elbows tagging along, somebody'll come up to you between your house and the waterfront. They'll have a handkerchief up to their face for a second, and then they'll let it fall to the ground.

'When you see that, you'll lay the money on the pavement, turn around, and walk back to your house. If the money isn't marked, and you don't try any fancy tricks, you'll get your daughter back in an hour or two. If you try to pull anything – remember what we wrote you! Got it straight?'

Gatewood sputtered something that was meant for an affirmative, and the telephone clicked silent.

I didn't waste any of my precious time tracing the call

– it would be from a public telephone. I knew – but yelled up the stairs to Gatewood, 'You do as you were told, and don't try any foolishness!'

Then I ran out into the early morning air to find the police detectives and the post office inspector.

They had been joined by two plainclothesmen, and had two automobiles waiting. I told them what the situation was, and we laid hurried plans.

O'Gar was to drive in one of the cars down Sacramento Street, and Thode, in the other, down Washington Street. These streets parallel Clay, one on each side. They were to drive slowly, keeping pace with Gatewood, and stopping at each cross street to see that he passed. When he failed to cross within a reasonable time they were to turn up to Clay Street – and their actions from then on would have to be guided by chance and their own wits.

Lusk was to wander along a block or two ahead of Gatewood, on the opposite side of the street, pretending to be mildly intoxicated.

I was to shadow Gatewood down the street, with one of the plainclothesmen behind me. The other plainclothesman was to turn in a call at headquarters for every available man to be sent to City Street. They would arrive too late, of course, and as likely as not it would take them some time to find us; but we had no way of knowing what was going to turn up before the night was over.

Our plan was sketchy enough, but it was the best we could do – we were afraid to grab whoever got the money from Gatewood. The girl's talk with her father that afternoon sounded too much as if her captors were desperate for us to take any chances on going after them roughshod until she was out of their hands.

We had hardly finished our plans when Gatewood, wearing a heavy overcoat, left his house and turned down the street.

Farther down, Lusk, weaving along, talking to himself, was almost invisible in the shadows. There was no one else in sight. That meant that I had to give Gatewood at least two blocks' lead, so that the man who came for the money wouldn't tumble to me. One of the plainclothesmen was half a block behind me, on the other side of the street.

We walked two blocks down, and then a chunky man in a derby hat came into sight. He passed Gatewood, passed me, went on.

Three blocks more.

A touring car, large, black, powerfully engined and with lowered curtains, came from the rear, passed us, went on. Possibly a scout. I scrawled its licence number down on my pad without taking my hand out of my overcoat pocket.

Another three blocks.

A policeman passed, strolling along in ignorance of the game being played under his nose; and then a taxicab with a single male passenger. I wrote down its licence number.

Four blocks with no one in sight ahead of me but Gatewood – I couldn't see Lusk any more.

Just ahead of Gatewood a man stepped out of a black doorway, turned around, called up to a window for someone to come down and open the door for him.

We went on.

Coming from nowhere, a woman stood on the sidewalk fifty feet ahead of Gatewood, a handkerchief to her face. It fluttered to the pavement.

Gatewood stopped, standing stifflegged. I could see his right hand come up, lifting the side of the overcoat in which it was pocketed – and I knew his hand was gripped around a pistol.

For perhaps half a minute he stood like a statue. Then his left hand came out of his pocket, and the bundle of money fell to the sidewalk in front of him, where it made a bright blur in the darkness. Gatewood turned abruptly, and began to retrace his steps homeward.

The woman had recovered her handkerchief. Now she ran to the bundle, picked it up, and scuttled to the black mouth of an alley a few feet distant – a rather tall woman, bent, and in dark clothes from head to feet.

In the black mouth of the alley she vanished.

I had been compelled to slow up while Gatewood and the woman stood facing each other, and I was more than a block away now. As soon as the woman disappeared,

I took a chance and started pounding my rubber shoes against the pavement.

The alley was empty when I reached it.

It ran all the way through to the next street, but I knew that the woman couldn't have reached the other end before I got to this one. I carry a lot of weight these days, but I can still step a block or two in good time. Along both sides of the alley were the rears of apartment buildings, each with its back door looking blankly, secretively, at me.

The plainclothesman who had been trailing behind me came up, then O'Gar and Thode in their cars, and soon, Lusk. O'Gar and Thode rode off immediately to wind through the neighbouring streets, hunting for the woman. Lusk and the plainclothesman each planted himself on a corner from which two of the streets enclosing the block could be watched.

I went through the alley, hunting vainly for an unlocked door, an open window, a fire escape that would show recent use – any of the signs that a hurried departure from the alley might leave.

Nothing!

O'Gar came back shortly with some reinforcements from headquarters that he had picked up, and Gatewood.

Gatewood was burning.

'Bungled the damn thing again! I won't pay your agency a nickel, and I'll see that some of these so-called detectives get put back in a uniform and set to walking beats!'

'What'd the woman look like?' I asked him.

'I don't know! I thought you were hanging around to take care of her! She was old and bent, kind of, I guess, but I couldn't see her face for her veil. I don't know! What the hell were you men doing? It's a damned outrage the way . . .'

I finally got him quieted down and took him home, leaving the city men to keep the neighbourhood under surveillance. There were fourteen or fifteen of them on the job now, and every shadow held at least one.

The girl would head for home as soon as she was released and I wanted to be there to pump her. There was an excellent chance of catching her abductors before they got very far, if she could tell us anything at all about them.

Home, Gatewood went up against the whisky bottle again, while I kept one ear cocked at the telephone and the other at the front door. O'Gar or Thode phoned every half hour or so to ask if we'd heard from the girl.

They had still found nothing.

At 9 o'clock they, with Lusk, arrived at the house. The woman in black had turned out to be a man and got away.

In the rear of one of the apartment buildings that touched the alley – just a foot or so within the back door – they found a woman's skirt, long coat, hat and veil – all black. Investigating the occupants of the house, they had learned that an apartment had been rented to a young man named Leighton three days before.

Leighton was not home, when they went up to his apartment. His rooms held a lot of cold cigarette butts, an empty bottle, and nothing else that had not been there when he rented it.

The inference was clear; he had rented the apartment so that he might have access to the building. Wearing women's clothes over his own, he had gone out of the back door – leaving it unlatched behind him – to meet Gatewood. Then he had run back into the building, discarded his disguise and hurried through the building, out the front door, and away before we had our feeble net around the block – perhaps dodging into dark doorways here and there to avoid O'Gar and Thode in their cars.

Leighton, it seemed, was a man of about thirty, slender, about five feet eight or nine inches tall, with dark hair and eyes; rather good-looking, and well-dressed on the two occasions when people living in the building had seen him, in a brown suit and a light brown felt hat.

There was no possibility, according to both of the detectives and the post office inspector, that the girl might have been held, even temporarily, in Leighton's apartment.

Ten o'clock came, and no word from the girl.

Gatewood had lost his domineering bullheadedness by now and was breaking up. The suspense was getting him, and the liquor he had put away wasn't helping him. I didn't like him either personally or by reputation, but this morning I felt sorry for him.

I talked to the Agency over the phone and got the reports of the operatives who had been looking up Audrey's friends. The last person to see her had been an Agnes Dangerfield, who had seen her walking down Market Street near Sixth, alone, on the night of her abduction – some time between 8.15 and 8.45. Audrey had been too far away from the Dangerfield girl to speak to her.

For the rest, the boys had learned nothing except that Audrey was a wild, spoiled youngster who hadn't shown any great care in selecting her friends – just the sort of girl who could easily fall into the hands of a mob of highbinders.

Noon struck. No sign of the girl. We told the newspapers to turn loose the story, with the added developments of the past few hours.

Gatewood was broken; he sat with his head in his hands, looking at nothing. Just before I left to follow a hunch I had, he looked up at me, and I'd never have recognized him if I hadn't seen the change take place.

'What do you think is keeping her away?' he asked.

I didn't have the heart to tell him what I had every reason to suspect, now that the money had been paid and she had failed to show up. So I stalled with some vague assurances and left.

I caught a cab and dropped off in the shopping district. I visited the five largest department stores, going to all the women's wear departments from shoes to hats, and trying to learn if a man – perhaps one answering Leighton's description – had been buying clothes in the past couple of days that would fit Audrey Gatewood.

Failing to get any results, I turned the rest of the local stores over to one of the boys from the Agency, and went across the bay to canvass the Oakland stores.

At the first one I got action. A man who might easily have been Leighton had been in the day before, buying clothes of Audrey's size. He had bought lots of them, everything from lingerie to a coat, and – my luck was hitting all cylinders – had had his purchases delivered to T. Offord, at an address on Fourteenth Street.

At the Fourteenth Street address, an apartment house, I found Mr and Mrs Theodore Offord's names in the vestibule for Apartment 202.

I had just found the apartment number when the front door opened and a stout, middle-aged woman in a gingham housedress came out. She looked at me a bit curiously, so I asked, 'Do you know where I can find the superintendent?'

'I'm the superintendent,' she said.

I handed her a card and stepped indoors with her. 'I'm from the bonding department of the North American Casualty Company' – a repetition of the lie that was printed on the card I had given her – 'and a bond for Mr Offord has been applied for. Is he all right so far as you know?' With the slightly apologetic air of one going through with a necessary but not too important formality.

'A bond? That's funny He is going away tomorrow.'

'Well, I can't say what the bond is for,' I said lightly. 'We investigators just get the names and addresses. It may be for his present employer, or perhaps the man he is going to work for has applied for it. Or some firms have us look up prospective employees before they hire them, just to be safe.'

'Mr Offord, so far as I know, is a very nice young man,' she said, 'but he has been here only a week.'

'Not staying long, then?'

'No. They came here from Denver, intending to stay, but the low altitude doesn't agree with Mrs Offord, so they are going back.'

'Are you sure they came from Denver?'

'Well, they told me they did.'

'How many of them are there?'

'Only the two of them; they're young people.'

'Well, how do they impress you?' I asked, trying to get over the impression that I thought her a woman of shrewd judgement.

'They seem to be a very nice young couple. You'd

hardly know they were in their apartment most of the time, they're so quiet. I'm sorry they can't stay?'

'Do they go out much?'

'I really don't know. They have their keys, and unless I should happen to pass them going in or out I'd never see them.'

'Then, as a matter of fact you couldn't say whether they stayed away all night some nights or not. Could you?'

She eyed me doubtfully – I was stepping way over my pretext now, but I didn't think it mattered – and shook her head. 'No, I couldn't say.'

'They have many visitors?'

'I don't know. Mr Offord is not –'

She broke off as a man came in quietly from the street, brushed past me, and started to mount the steps to the second floor.

'Oh dear!' she whispered. 'I hope he didn't hear me talking about him. That's Mr Offord.'

A slender man in brown, with a light brown hat – Leighton, perhaps.

I hadn't seen anything of him except his back, nor he anything except mine. I watched him as he climbed the stairs. If he had heard the woman mention his name he would use the turn at the head of the stairs to sneak a look at me.

He did.

I kept my face stolid, but I knew him.

He was 'Penny' Quayle, a con man who had been active in the east four or five years before.

His face was as expressionless as mine. But he knew me.

A door on the second floor shut. I left the woman and started for the stairs.

'I think I'll go up and talk to him,' I told her.

Coming silently to the door of Apartment 202, I listened. Not a sound. This was no time for hesitation. I pressed the bell-button.

As close together as the tapping of three keys under the fingers of an expert typist, but a thousand times more vicious, came three pistol shots. And waist-high in the door of Apartment 202 were three bullet holes.

The three bullets would have been in my fat carcass if I hadn't learned years ago to stand to one side of strange doors when making uninvited calls.

Inside the apartment sounded a man's voice, sharp, commanding. 'Cut it, kid! For God's sake, not that!'

A woman's voice, shrill, bitter, spiteful, screaming blasphemies.

Two more bullets came through the door.

'Stop! No! No!' The man's voice had a note of fear in it now.

The woman's voice, cursing hotly. A scuffle. A shot that didn't hit the door.

I hurled my foot against the door, near the knob, and the lock broke away.

On the floor of the room, a man – Quayle – and a woman were tussling. He was bending over her, holding her wrists, trying to keep her down. A smoking pistol was in one of her hands. I got to it in a jump and tore it loose.

'That's enough!' I called to them when I was planted. 'Get up and receive company.'

Quayle released his antagonist's wrists, whereupon she struck at his eyes with curved, sharp-nailed fingers, tearing his cheek open. He scrambled away from her on hands and knees, and both of them got to their feet.

He sat down on a chair immediately, panting and wiping his bleeding cheek with a handkerchief.

She stood, hands on hips, in the centre of the room, glaring at me. 'I suppose,' she spat, 'you think you've raised hell!'

I laughed – I could afford to.

'If your father is in his right mind,' I told her, 'he'll do it with a razor strap when he gets you home again. A fine joke you picked out to play on him!'

'If *you'd* been tied to him as long as I have and had been bullied and held down as much, I guess *you'd* do most anything to get enough money so that you could go away and live your own life.'

I didn't say anything to that. Remembering some of the business methods Harvey Gatewood had used – particularly some of his war contracts that the Department of Justice was still investigating – I suppose the worst that could be said about Audrey was that she was her father's own daughter.

'How'd you rap to it?' Quayle asked me, politely.

'Several ways,' I said. 'First, one of Audrey's friends saw her on Market Street between 8.15 and 8.45 the night she disappeared and your letter to Gatewood was postmarked 9 p.m. Pretty fast work. You should have waited a while before mailing it. I suppose she dropped it in the post office on her way over here?'

Quayle nodded.

'Then second,' I went on, 'there was that phone call of hers. She knew it took anywhere from ten to fifteen minutes to get her father on the wire at the office. If she had gotten to a phone while imprisoned, time would have been so valuable that she'd have told her story to the first person she got hold of – the switchboard operator, most likely. So that made it look as if, besides wanting to throw out that Twin Peaks line, she wanted to stir the old man out of his bullheadedness.

'When she failed to show up after the money was paid, I figured it was a sure bet that she had kidnapped herself. I knew that if she came back home after faking this thing, we'd find it out before we'd talked to her very long – and I figured she knew that too and would stay away.

'The rest was easy – I got some good breaks. We knew a man was working with her after we found the woman's clothes you left behind, and I took a chance on there being no one else in it. Then I figured she'd need clothes – she couldn't have taken any from home without tipping her mitt – and there was an even chance that she hadn't laid in a stock beforehand. She's got too many girl friends of the sort that do a lot of shopping to make it safe for her to have risked showing herself in stores. Maybe, then, the man would buy what she needed. And it turned out that he did, and that he was too lazy to carry away his purchases, or perhaps there were too many of them, and so he had them sent out. That's the story.'

Quayle nodded again.

'I was damned careless,' he said, and then, jerking a contemptuous thumb toward the girl. 'But what can you expect? She's had a skinful of hop ever since we started. Took all my time and attention keeping her from running wild and gumming the works. Just now was a sample – I told her you were coming up and she goes crazy and tries to add your corpse to the wreckage!'

The Gatewood reunion took place in the office of the captain of inspectors on the second floor of the Oakland City Hall, and it was a merry little party.

For over an hour it was a tossup whether Harvey Gatewood would die of apoplexy, strangle his daughter or send her off to the state reformatory until she was of age. But Audrey licked him. Besides being a chip off the old block, she was young enough to be careless of consequences, while her father, for all his bullheadedness, had had some caution hammered into him.

The card she beat him with was a threat of spilling everything she knew about him to the newspapers, and at least one of the San Francisco papers had been trying to get his scalp for years.

I don't know what she had on him, and I don't think he was any too sure himself; but with his war contracts still being investigated by the Department of Justice, he couldn't afford to take a chance. There was no doubt at all that she would have done as she threatened.

And so, together, they left for home, sweating hate for each other from every pore.

We took Quayle upstairs and put him in a cell, but he was too experienced to let that worry him. He knew that if the girl was to be spared, he himself couldn't very easily be convicted of anything.

I was glad it was over. It had been a tough caper.

To Have and Have Not-Harry Morgan

Ernest Hemingway

Albert was on board the boat and the gas was loaded.

'I'll start her up and try how those two cylinders hit,' Harry said. 'You got the things stowed?'

'Yes.'

'Cut some baits then.'

'You want a wide bait?'

'That's right. For tarpon.'

Albert was on the stern cutting baits and Harry was at the wheel warming up the motors when he heard a noise like a motor backfiring. He looked down the street and saw a man come out of the bank. He had a gun in his hand and he came running. Then he was out of sight. Two more men came out carrying leather brief cases and guns in their hands and ran in the same direction. Harry looked at Albert busy cutting baits. The fourth man, the big one, came out of the bank door as he watched, holding a Thompson gun in front of him, and as he backed out of the door the siren in the bank rose in a long breath-taking shriek and Harry saw the gun muzzle jump-jump-jump-jump and heard the bop-bop-bop-bop, small and hollow sounding in the wail of the siren. This man turned and ran, stopping to fire once more at the bank door, and Albert stood up in the stern saying, 'Christ, they're robbing the bank. Christ, what can we do?' Harry heard the Ford taxi coming out of the side street and saw it careening up on to the dock.

There were three Cubans in the back and one beside the driver.

'Where's the boat?' yelled one in Spanish.

'There, you fool,' said another.

'That's not the boat.'

'That's the captain.'

'Come on. Come on for Christ sake.'

'Get out,' said the Cuban to the driver. 'Get your hands up.'

As the driver stood beside the car he put a knife inside his belt and ripping it toward him cut the belt and slit his pants almost to the knee. He yanked the trousers down. 'Stand still,' he said. The two Cubans with the valises tossed them into the cockpit of the launch and they all came tumbling aboard.

'Geta going,' said one. The big one with the machine-gun poked it into Harry's back.

'Come on, Cappie,' he said, 'Let's go.'

'Take it easy,' said Harry. 'Point that some place else.'

'Cast off those lines,' the big one said. 'You!' to Albert.

'Wait a minute,' Albert said. 'Don't start her. These are the bank robbers.'

The biggest Cuban turned and swung the Thompson gun and held it on Albert. 'Hey, don't! Don't!' Albert said. 'Don't!'

The burst was so close to his chest that the bullets whocked like three slaps. Albert slid down on his knees, his eyes wide, his mouth open. He looked like he was still trying to say, 'Don't!'

'You don't need no mate,' the big Cuban said. 'You one-armed son-of-a-bitch.' Then in Spanish. 'Cut those lines with that fish knife.' And in English, 'Come on. Let's go.'

Then in Spanish, 'Put a gun against his back!' and in English, 'Come on. Let's go. I'll blow your head off.'

'We'll go,' said Harry.

One of the Indian-looking Cubans was holding a pistol against the side his bad arm was on. The muzzle almost touched the hook.

As he swung her out, spinning the wheel with his good arm, he looked astern to watch the clearance past the piling, and saw Albert on his knees in the stern, his head slipped sidewise now, in a pool of it. On the dock was the Ford taxi, and the fat driver in his under-drawers, his trousers around his ankles, his hands above his head, his mouth open as wide as Albert's. There was still no one coming down the street.

The pilings of the dock went past as she came out of the basin and then he was in the channel passing the lighthouse dock.

'Come on. Hook her up,' the big Cuban said. 'Make some time.'

'Take that gun away,' Harry said. He was thinking, I could run her on Crawfish bar, but sure as hell that Cuban would plug me.

'Make her go,' said the big Cuban. Then, in Spanish, 'Lie down flat, everybody. Keep the captain covered.' He lay down himself in the stern, pulling Albert flat down into the cockpit. The other three all lay flat in the cockpit now. Harry sat on the steering seat. He was looking ahead steering out the channel, past the opening into the sub-base now, with the notice board to yachts and the green blinker, out away from the jetty, past the red blinker; he looked back. The big Cuban had a green box of shells out of his pocket and was filling clips. The gun lay by his side and he was filling clips without looking at them, filling by feel, looking back over the stern. The others were all looking astern except the one that was watching him. This one, one of the two Indian-looking ones, motioned with his pistol for him to look ahead. No boat had started after them yet. The engines were running smoothly and they were going with the tide. He noticed the heavy slant seawards of the buoy he passed, with the current swirling at its base.

There are two speedboats that could catch us, Harry was thinking. One, Ray's, is running the mail from Matecumbe. Where is the other? I saw her a couple of days ago on Ed Taylor's ways, he checked. That was the one I thought of having Bee-lips hire. There's two more, he remembered now. One the State Road Department has up along the keys. The other's laid up in the Garrison Bight. How far are we now? He looked back to where the fort was well astern, the red-brick building of the old post office starting to show up above the navy yard buildings and the yellow hotel building now dominating the short skyline of the town. There was the cove at the fort, and the lighthouse showed above the houses that strung out towards the big winter hotel. Four miles anyway, he thought. There they come, he thought. Two white fishing boats were rounding the breakwater and heading out toward him. They can't do ten, he thought. It's pitiful.

The Cubans were chattering in Spanish.

'How fast you going, Cappie?' the big one said, looking back from the stern.

'About twelve,' Harry said.

'What can those boats do?'

'Maybe ten.'

They were all watching them now, even the one who was supposed to keep him, Harry, covered. But what can I do? He thought. Nothing to do yet.

The two white boats got no larger.

'Look at that, Roberto,' said the nice-speaking one.

'Where?'

'Look!'

A long way back, so far you could hardly see it, a little spout rose in the water.

'They shooting at us,' the pleasant-speaking one said. 'It's silly.'

'For Christ's sake,' the big-faced one said. 'At three miles.'

'Four,' thought Harry. 'All of four.'

Harry could see the tiny spouts rise on the calm surface but he could not hear the shots.

'Those Conch's are pitiful,' he thought. 'They're worse. They're comical.'

'What government boat is there, Cappie?' asked the big-faced one looking away from the stern.

'Coastguard.'

'What can she make?'

'Maybe twelve.'

'Then we're O.K. now?'

Harry did not answer.

'Aren't we O.K. then?'

Harry said nothing. He was keeping the rising, widening spire of Sand Key on his left and the stake on little Sand Key shoals showed almost abeam to starboard. In ten more minutes they would be past the reef.

'What's the matter with you? Can't you talk?'

'What did you ask me?'

'Is there anything can catch us now?'

‘Coastguard plane,’ said Harry.

‘We cut the telephone wire before we came in town,’ the pleasant-speaking one said.

‘You didn’t cut the wireless, did you?’ Harry asked.

‘You think the plane can get here?’

‘You got a chance of her until dark,’ Harry said.

‘What do you think, Cappie?’ asked Roberto, the big-faced one.

Harry did not answer.

‘Come on, what do you think?’

‘What did you let that son of a bitch kill my mate for?’ Harry said to the pleasant-speaking one who was standing beside him now looking at the compass course.

‘Shut up,’ said Roberto. ‘Kill you, too.’

‘How much money you get?’ Harry asked the pleasant-speaking one.

‘We don’t know. We haven’t counted it yet. It isn’t ours, anyway.’

‘I guess not,’ said Harry. He was past the light now and he put on 225°, his regular course for Havana.

‘I mean we do it not for ourselves. For a revolutionary organization.’

‘You kill my mate for that, too?’

‘I am very sorry,’ said the boy. ‘I cannot tell you how badly I feel about that.’

‘Don’t try,’ said Harry.

‘You see,’ the boy said, speaking quietly, ‘this man Roberto is bad. He is a good revolutionary but a bad man. He kills so much in the time of Machado he gets to like it. He thinks it is funny to kill. He kills in a good cause, of course. The best cause.’ He looked back at Roberto who sat now in one of the fishing chairs in the stern, the Thompson gun across his lap, looking back at the white boats which were, Harry saw, much smaller now.

‘What you got to drink?’ Roberto called from the stern.

‘Nothing,’ Harry said.

‘I drink my own, then,’ Roberto said. One of the other Cubans lay on one of the seats built over the gas tanks. He looked seasick already. The other was obviously seasick too, still sitting up.

Looking back, Harry saw a lead-coloured boat, now clear of the fort, coming up on the two white boats.

'There's the coastguard boat,' he thought. 'She's pitiful too.'

'You think the seaplane will come?' the pleasant-spoken boy asked.

'Be dark in half an hour,' Harry said. He settled on the steering seat. 'What you figure on doing? Killing me?'

'I don't want to,' the boy said. 'I hate killing.'

'What you doing?' Roberto, who sat now with a pint of whisky in his hand asked. 'Making friends with the captain? What you want to do? Eat at the captain's table?'

'Take the wheel,' Harry said to the boy. 'See the course? Two twenty-five.' He straightened up from the stool and went aft.

'Let me have a drink,' Harry said to Roberto. 'There's your coastguard boat but she can't catch us.'

He had abandoned anger, hatred, and any dignity as luxuries, now, and had started to plan.

'Sure,' said Roberto. 'She can't catch us. Look at those seasick babies. What you say? You want a drink? You got any other last wishes, Cappie?'

'You're some kidder,' Harry said. He took a long drink.

'Go easy!' Roberto protested. 'That's all there is.'

'I got some more,' Harry told him. 'I was just kidding you.'

'Don't kid me,' said Roberto suspiciously.

'Why should I try?'

'What you got?'

'Bacardi.'

'Bring it out.'

'Take it easy,' Harry said. 'Why do you get so tough?'

He stepped over Albert's body as he walked forward. As he came to the wheel he looked at the compass. The boy was about twenty-five degrees off and the compass dial was swinging. He's no sailor, Harry thought. That gives me more time. Look at the wake.

The wake ran in two bubbling curves toward where the light, astern now, showed brown, conical, and thinly latticed on the horizon. The boats were almost out of sight. He could just see a blur where the wireless masts of the town were. The engines were running smoothly. Harry put his head below and reached for one of the bottles of Bacardi. He went aft with it. At the stern he took a drink, then handed the bottle to Roberto. Standing, he looked down at Albert and he felt sick inside. The poor hungry bastard, he thought.

'What's the matter? He scare you?' the big-faced Cuban asked.

'What you say we put him over?' Harry said. 'No sense to carry him.'

'O.K.' said Roberto. 'You got good sense.'

'Take him under the arms,' said Harry. 'I'll take the legs.' Roberto laid the Thompson gun down on the wide stern and leaning down lifted the body by the shoulders.

'You know the heaviest thing in the world is a dead man,' he said. 'You ever lift a dead man before. Cappie?'

'No,' said Harry. 'You ever lift a big dead woman?'

Roberto pulled the body up on to the stern. 'You're a tough fellow,' he said. 'What do you say we have a drink?'

'Go ahead,' said Harry.

'Listen, I'm sorry I killed him,' Roberto said. 'When I kill you I feel worse.'

'Cut out talking that way,' Harry said. 'What do you want to talk that way for?'

'Come on,' said Roberto. 'Over he goes.'

As they leaned over and slid the body up and over the stern, Harry kicked the machine-gun over the edge. It splashed at the same time Albert did, but while Albert turned over twice in the white, churned, bubbling back-suction of the propellor wash before sinking, the gun went straight down.

'That's better, eh?' Roberto said. 'Make it shipshape.' Then as he saw the gun was gone, 'Where is it? What did you do with it?'

'With what?'

'The *ametralladora!*' going into Spanish in excitement.

'The what?'

'You know what.'

'I didn't see it.'

'You knocked it off the stern. Now I'll kill you, *now.*'

'Take it easy,' said Harry. 'What the hell you going to kill me about?'

'Give me a gun,' Roberto said to one of the seasick Cubans in Spanish. 'Give me a gun quick!'

Harry stood there, never having felt so tall, never having felt so wide, feeling the sweat trickle from under his armpits, feeling it go down his flanks.

'You kill too much,' he heard the seasick Cuban say in Spanish. 'You kill the mate. Now you want to kill the captain. Who's going to get us across?'

'Leave him alone,' said the other. 'Kill him when we get over.'

'He knocked the machine-gun over board,' Roberto said.

'We got the money. What you want a machine-gun for now? There's plenty of machine-guns in Cuba.'

'I tell you, you make a mistake if you don't kill him now, I tell you. Give me a gun.'

'Oh, shut up. You're drunk. Every time you're drunk you want to kill somebody.'

'Have a drink,' said Harry looking out across the grey swell of the Gulf Stream where the round red sun was just touching the water. 'Watch that. When she goes all the way under it'll turn bright green.'

'The hell with that,' said the big-faced Cuban. 'You think you got away with something.'

'I'll get you another gun,' said Harry. 'They only cost forty-five dollars in Cuba. Take it easy. You're all right now. There ain't any coastguard plane going to come now.'

'I'm going to kill you,' Roberto said, looking him over. 'You did that on purpose. That's why you got me to lift on that.'

'You don't want to kill me,' Harry said. 'Who's going to take you across?'

'I ought to kill you now.'

'Take it easy,' said Harry. 'I'm going to look at the engines.'

He opened the hatch, got down in, screwed down the grease cups on the two stuffing boxes, felt the motors, and with his hand touched the butt of the Thompson gun. Not yet, he thought. No, better not yet. Christ, that was lucky. What the hell difference does it make to Albert when he's dead? Saves his old woman to bury him. That big-faced bastard. That big-faced murdering bastard. Christ, I'd like to take him now. But I better wait.

He stood up, climbed out and shut the hatch.

'How you doing?' he said to Roberto. He put his hand on the fat shoulder. The big-faced Cuban looked at him and did not say anything.

'Did you see it turn green?' Harry said.

'The hell with you,' Roberto said. He was drunk but he was suspicious, and, like an animal, he knew how wrong something had gone.

'Let me take her a while,' Harry said to the boy at the wheel. 'What's your name?'

'You can call me Emilio,' said the boy.

'Go below and you'll find something to eat,' Harry said. 'There's bread and corn-beef. Make coffee if you want.'

'I don't want any.'

'I'll make some later,' Harry said. He sat at the wheel, the binnacle light on now, holding her on the point easily in the light following sea, looking out at the night coming on the water. He had no running lights on.

It would be a pretty night to cross, he thought, a pretty night. Soon as the last of that afterglow is gone I've got to work her east. If I don't, we'll sight the glare of Havana in another hour. In two, anyway. Soon as he sees the glare it may occur to that son of a bitch to kill me. That was lucky getting rid of that gun. Damn, that was lucky. Wonder what that Marie's having for supper. I guess she's plenty worried. I guess she's too worried to eat. Wonder how much money those bastards have got. Funny they don't count it. If that ain't a hell of a way to raise money for a revolution. Cubans are a hell of a people.

That's a mean boy, that Roberto. I'll get him to-night. I get him no matter how the rest of it comes out. That won't help that poor damned Albert though. It made me feel bad to dump him like that. I don't know what made me think of it.

He lit a cigarette and smoked in the dark.

I'm doing all right, he thought. I'm doing better than I expected. The kid is a kind of nice kid. I wish I could get those other two on the same side. I wish there was some way to bunch them. Well, I'll have to do the best I can. Easier I can make them take it the better. Smoother everything goes the better.

'Do you want a sandwich?' the boy asked.

'Thanks,' said Harry. 'You give one to your partner?'

'He's drinking. He won't eat,' the boy said.

'What about the others?'

'Seasick,' the boy said.

'It's nice night to cross,' Harry said. He noticed the boy did not watch the compass so he kept letting her go off to the east.

'I'd enjoy it,' the boy said. 'If it wasn't for your mate.'

'He was a good fellow,' said Harry. 'Did any one get hurt at the bank?'

'The lawyer. What was his name, Simmons.'

'Get killed?'

'I think so.'

So, thought Harry. Mr Bee-lips. What the hell did he expect? How could he have thought he wouldn't get it? That comes from playing at being tough. That comes from being too smart too often. Mr Bee-lips. Good-bye, Mr Bee-lips.

'How he come to get killed?'

'I guess you can imagine,' the boy said. 'That's very different from your mate. I feel badly about that. You know he doesn't mean to do wrong. It's just what that phase of the revolution has done to him.'

'I guess he's probably a good fellow,' Harry said, and thought, Listen to what my mouth says. God damn it, my mouth will say anything. But I got to try to make a friend of this boy in case . . .

'What kind of revolution do you make now?' he asked.

'We are the only true revolutionary party,' the boy said. 'We want to do away with all the old politicians, with all the American imperialism that strangles us, with the tyranny of the army. We want to start clean and give every man a chance. We want to end the slavery of the *guajiros*, you know, the peasants, and divide the big sugar estates among the people that work them. But we are not Communists.'

Harry looked up from the compass card at him.

'How you coming on?' he asked.

'We just raise money now for the fight,' the boy said. 'To do that we have to use means that later we would never use. Also we have to use people we would not employ later. But the end is worth the means. They had to do the same thing in Russia. Stalin was a sort of brigand for many years before the revolution.'

He's a radical, Harry thought. That's what he is, a radical.

'I guess you've got a good programme,' he said, 'if you're out to help the working man. I was out on strike plenty times in the old days when we had the cigar factories in Key West. I'd have been glad to do whatever I could if I'd known what kind of outfit you were.'

'Lots of people would help us,' the boy said. 'But because of the state the movement is in at present we can't trust people. I regret the necessity for the present phase very much. I hate terrorism. I also feel very badly about the methods for raising the necessary money. But there is no choice. You do not know how bad things are in Cuba.'

'I guess they're plenty bad,' Harry said.

'You can't know how bad they are. There is an absolutely murderous tyranny that extends over every little village in the country. Three people cannot be together on the street. Cuba has no foreign enemies and doesn't need any army, but she has an army of twenty-five thousand now, and the army, from the corporals up, suck the blood from the nation. Everyone, even the private soldiers, are out to make their fortunes. Now they have a military reserve with every kind of crook, bully, and informer of the old days of Machado in it, and they take anything the army does not bother with. We have to get rid of the army before anything can start. Before we were ruled by clubs. Now we are ruled by rifles, pistols, machine-guns, and bayonets.'

'It sounds bad,' Harry said, steering, and letting her go off to the eastward.

'You cannot realize how bad it is,' the boy said. 'I love my poor country and I would do anything, anything to free it from this tyranny we have now. I do things I hate. But I would do things I hate a thousand times more.'

I want a drink, Harry was thinking. What the hell do I care about his revolution. F—— his revolution. To help the working man he robs a bank and kills a fellow works with him and then kills that poor damned Albert that never did any harm. That's a working man he kills. He never thinks of that. With a family. It's the Cubans run Cuba. They all double cross each other. They sell each other out. They get what they deserve. The hell with their revolutions. All I got to do is to make a living for my family and I can't do that. Then he tells me about his revolution. The hell with his revolution.

'It must be bad, all right,' he said to the boy. 'Take the wheel a minute, will you? I want to get a drink.'

'Sure,' said the boy. 'How should I steer?'

'Two twenty-five,' Harry said.

It was dark now and there was quite a swell this far out in the Gulf Stream. He passed the two seasick Cubans lying out on the seats and went aft to where Roberto sat in the fishing chair. The water was racing past the boat in the dark. Roberto sat with his feet in the other fishing chair that was turned toward him.

'Let me have some of that,' Harry said to him.

'Go to hell,' said the big-faced man thickly. 'This is mine.'

'All right,' said Harry, and went forward to get the other bottle. Below in the dark, with the bottle under the flap of his right arm, he pulled the cork that Freddy had drawn and reinserted and took a drink.

Now's as good as any time, he said to himself. No sense waiting now. Little boy's spoke his piece. The big-faced bastard drunk; the other two seasick. It might as well be now.

He took another drink and the Bacardi warmed and helped him but he felt cold and hollow all around his stomach still. His whole insides were cold.

'Want a drink?' he asked the boy at the wheel.

'No, thanks,' the boy said. 'I don't drink.' Harry could

see him smile in the binnacle light. He was a nice-looking boy all right. Pleasant talking, too.

'I'll take one,' he said. He swallowed a big one but it could not warm the dank cold part that had spread from his stomach to all over the inside of his chest now. He put the bottle down on the cockpit floor.

'Keep her on that course,' he said to the boy. 'I'm going to have a look at the motors.'

He opened the hatch and stepped down. Then locked the hatch up with a long hook that set into a hole in the flooring. He stooped over the motors, with his one hand felt the water manifold, the cylinders, and put his hand on the stuffing boxes. He tightened the two grease cups a turn and a half each. Quit stalling, he said to himself. Come on, quit stalling. Where're your balls now? Under my chin, I guess, he thought.

He looked out of the hatch. He could almost touch the two seats over the gas tanks where the seasick men lay. The boy's back was toward him, sitting on the high stool, outlined clearly by the binnacle light. Turning, he could see Roberto sprawled in the chair in the stern, silhouetted against the dark water.

Twenty-one to a clip is four bursts of five at the most, he thought. I got to be light-fingered. All right. Come on. Quit stalling, you gutless wonder. Christ, what I'd give for another one. Well, there isn't any other one now. He reached his left hand up, unhooked the length of belting, put his hand around the trigger guard, pushed the safety all the way over with his thumb and pulled the gun out. Squatting in the engine pit he sighted carefully on the back of the boy's head where it outlined against the light from the binnacle.

The gun made a big flame in the dark and the shells rattled against the lifted hatch and on to the engine. Before the slump of the boy's body fell from the stool he had turned and shot into the figure on the left bunk, holding the jerking, flame-stabbing gun almost against the man, so close he could smell it burn his coat; then swung to put a burst into the other bunk where the man was sitting up, tugging at his pistol. He crouched low now and looked astern. The big-faced man was gone out of the chair. He could see both chairs silhouetted.

Behind him the boy lay still. There wasn't any doubt about him. On one bunk a man was flopping. On the other, he could see with the corner of his eye, a man lay half over the gunwale, fallen over on his face.

Harry was trying to locate the big-faced man in the dark. The boat was going in a circle now and the cockpit lightened a little. He held his breath and looked. That must be him where it was a little darker on the floor in the corner. He watched it and it moved a little. That was him.

The man was crawling toward him. No, toward the man who lay half overboard. He was after his gun. Crouching low, Harry watched him move until he was absolutely sure. Then he gave him a burst. The gun lighted him on hands and knees, and, as the flame and the bot-bot-bot-bot stopped, he heard him flopping heavily.

'You son of a bitch,' said Harry. 'You big-faced murdering bastard.'

All the cold was gone from around his heart now and he had the old hollow, singing feeling and he crouched low down and felt under the square, wood-crated gas tank for another clip to put in the gun. He got the clip, but his hand was cold-drying wet.

Hit the tank, he said to himself. I've got to cut the engines. I don't know where that tank cuts.

He pressed the curved lever, dropped the empty clip, shoved in the fresh one, and climbed up and out of the cockpit.

As he stood up, holding the Thompson gun in his left hand, looking around before shutting the hatch with the hook on his right arm, the Cuban who had lain on the port bunk and had been shot three times through the left shoulder, two shots going into the gas tank, sat up, took careful aim, and shot him in the belly.

Harry sat down in a backward lurch. He felt as though he had been struck in the abdomen with a club. His back was against one of the iron-pipe supports of the fishing chairs and while the Cuban shot at him again and splintered the fishing chair above his head, he reached down, found the Thompson gun, raised it carefully, holding the forward grip with the hook and rattled half of the fresh clip into the man who sat leaning forward, calmly shooting at him from the seat. The man was down on the seat in a heap and Harry felt around on the cockpit floor until he could find the big-faced man, who lay face down, felt for his head with the hook on his bad arm, hooked it around, then put the muzzle of the gun against the head and touched the trigger. Touching the head, the gun made a noise like hitting a pumpkin with a club. Harry put down the gun and lay on his side on the cockpit floor.

'I'm a son of a bitch,' he said, his lips against the planking. I'm a gone son of a bitch now. I got to cut the engines or we'll all burn up, he thought. I got a chance still. I got a kind of a chance. Jesus Christ. One thing to spoil it. One thing to go wrong. God damn it. Oh, God *damn* that Cuban bastard. Who'd have thought I hadn't got him?

He got on his hands and knees and letting one side of the hatch over the engines slam down, crawled over it forward to where the steering stool was. He pulled up on it, surprised to find how well he could move, then suddenly feeling faint and weak as he stood erect, he leaned forward with his bad arm resting on the compass and cut the two switches. The engines were quiet and he could hear the water against her sides. There was no other sound. She swung into the trough of the little sea the North wind had raised and began to roll.

He hung against the wheel, then eased himself on to the steering stool, leaning against the chart table. He could feel the strength drain out of him in a steady faint nausea. He opened his shirt with his good hand and felt the hole with the base of the palm of his hand, then fingered it. There was very little bleeding. All inside, he thought. I better lie down and give it a chance to quiet.

The moon was up now and he could see what was in the cockpit.

Some mess, he thought, some hell of a mess.

Better get down before I fall down, he thought and he lowered himself down to the cockpit floor.

He lay on his side and then, as the boat rolled, the moonlight came in and he could see everything in the cockpit clearly.

It's crowded, he thought. That's what it is, it's crowded. Then, he thought, I wonder what she'll do. I wonder what Marie will do? Maybe they'll pay her the rewards. God damn that Cuban. She'll get along, I guess. She's a smart woman. I guess we would all have gotten along. I guess it was nuts all right. I guess I bit off too much more than I could chew. I shouldn't have tried it. I had it all right up to the end. Nobody'll know how it happened. I wish I could do something about Marie. Plenty money on this boat. I don't even know how much. Anybody be O.K. with that money. I wonder if the coastguard will pinch it. Some of it, I guess. I wish I could let the old woman know what happened. I wonder what she'll do? I don't know. I guess I should have got a job in a filling station or something. I should have quit trying to go in boats. There's no honest money going in boats any more. If the bitch wouldn't only roll. If she'd only quit rolling. I can feel all that slopping back and forth inside. Me. Mr Bee-lips and Albert. Everybody that had to do with it. These bastards too. It must be an unlucky business. Some unlucky business. I guess what a man like me ought to do is run something like a filling station. Hell, I couldn't run no filling station. Marie, she'll run something. She's too old to peddle her hips now. I wish this bitch wouldn't roll. I'll just have to take it easy. I got to take it as easy as I can. They say if you don't drink water and lay still. They say especially if you don't drink water.

He looked at what the moonlight showed in the cockpit.

Well, I don't have to clean her up, he thought. Take it easy. That's what I got to do. Take it easy. I've got to take it as easy as I can. I've got sort of a chance. If you lay still and don't drink any water.

He lay on his back and tried to breathe steadily. The launch rolled in the Gulf Stream swell and Harry Morgan lay on his back in the cockpit. At first he tried to brace himself against the roll with his good hand. Then he lay quietly and took it.

I'll Be Waiting

Raymond Chandler

At one o'clock in the morning, Carl, the night porter, turned down the last of three table lamps in the main lobby of the Windermere Hotel. The blue carpet darkened a shade or two and the walls drew back into remoteness. The chairs filled with shadowy loungers. In the corners were memories like cobwebs.

Tony Reseck yawned. He put his head on one side and listened to the frail, twittery music from the radio room beyond a dim arch at the far side of the lobby. He frowned. That should be his radio room after one a.m. Nobody should be in it. That red-haired girl was spoiling his nights.

The frown passed and a miniature of a smile quirked at the corners of his lips. He sat relaxed, a short, pale, paunchy, middle-aged man with long, delicate fingers clasped on the elk's tooth on his watch chain; the long delicate fingers of a sleight-of-hand artist, fingers with shiny, moulded nails and tapering first joints, fingers a little spatulate at the ends. Handsome fingers. Tony Reseck rubbed them gently together and there was peace in his quiet sea-grey eyes.

The frown came back on his face. The music annoyed him. He got up with a curious litheness, all in one piece, without moving his clasped hands from the watch chain. At one moment he was leaning back relaxed, and the next he was standing balanced on his feet, perfectly still, so that the movement of rising seemed to be a thing imperfectly perceived, an error of vision.

He walked with small, polished shoes delicately across the blue carpet and under the arch. The music was louder. It contained the hot, acid blare, the frenetic, jittering runs of a jam session. It was too loud. The red-haired girl sat there and stared silently at the fretted part of the big radio cabinet as though she could see the band with its fixed professional grin and the sweat running down its back. She was curled up with her feet under her on a davenport which seemed to contain most of the cushions in the room. She was tucked among them carefully, like a corsage in the florist's tissue paper.

She didn't turn her head. She leaned there, one hand in a small fist on her peach-coloured knee. She was wearing lounging pyjamas of heavy ribbed silk embroidered with black lotus buds.

'You like Goodman, Miss Cressy?' Tony Reseck asked.

The girl moved her eyes slowly. The light in there was dim, but the violet of her eyes almost hurt. They were large, deep eyes without a trace of thought in them. Her face was classical and without expression.

She said nothing.

Tony smiled and moved his fingers at his sides, one by one, feeling them move. 'You like Goodman, Miss Cressy?' he repeated gently.

'Not to cry over,' the girl said tonelessly.

Tony rocked back on his heels and looked at her eyes.

Large, deep, empty eyes. Or were they? He reached down and muted the radio.

'Don't get me wrong,' the girl said. 'Goodman makes money, and a lad that makes legitimate money these days is a lad you have to respect. But this jitterbug music gives me the backdrop of a beer flat. I like something with roses in it.'

'Maybe you like Mozart,' Tony said.

'Go on, kid me,' the girl said.

'I wasn't kidding you, Miss Cressy, I think Mozart was the greatest man that ever lived – and Toscanini is his prophet.'

'I thought you were the house dick.' She put her head back on a pillow and stared at him through her lashes. 'Make me some of that Mozart,' she added.

'It's too late,' Tony sighed. 'You can't get it now.'

She gave him another long lucid glance. 'Got the eye on me, haven't you, flatfoot?' She laughed a little, almost under her breath. 'What did I do wrong?'

Tony smiled his toy smile. 'Nothing, Miss Cressy. Nothing at all. But you need some fresh air. You've been five days in this hotel and you haven't been outdoors. And you have a tower room.'

She laughed again. 'Make me a story about it. I'm bored.'

'There was a girl here once had your suite. She stayed in the hotel a whole week, like you. Without going out at all, I mean. She didn't speak to anybody hardly. What do you think she did then?'

The girl eyed him gravely. 'She jumped her bill.'

He put his long delicate hand out and turned it slowly, fluttering the fingers, with an effect almost like a lazy wave breaking. 'Uh-uh. She sent down for her bill and paid it. Then she told the hop to be back in half an hour for her suitcases. Then she went out on her balcony.'

The girl leaned forward a little, her eyes still grave, one hand capping her peach-coloured knee. 'What did you say your name was?'

'Tony Reseck.'

'Sounds like a hunky.'

'Yeah,' Tony said. 'Polish.'

'Go on, Tony.'

'All the tower suites have private balconies, Miss Cressy. The walls of them are too low for fourteen stories above the street. It was a dark night, high clouds.' He dropped his hand with a final gesture, a farewell gesture. 'Nobody saw her jump. But when she hit, it was like a big gun going off.'

'You're making it up, Tony.' Her voice was a clean dry whisper of sound.

He smiled his toy smile. His quiet sea-green eyes seemed almost to be smoothing the long waves of her hair. 'Eve Cressy,' he said musingly. 'A name waiting for lights to be in.'

'Waiting for a tall dark guy that's no good, Tony. You wouldn't care why. I was married to him once. I might be married to him again. You can make a lot of mistakes in just one lifetime.' The hand on her knee opened slowly until the fingers were strained back as far as they would go. Then they closed quickly and tightly, and even in that dim light the knuckles shone like little polished stones. 'I played him a low trick once. I put him in a bad place – without meaning to. You wouldn't care about that either. It's just that I owe him something.'

He leaned over softly and turned the knob on the radio. A waltz formed itself dimly on the warm air. A tinsel waltz, but a waltz. He turned the volume up. The music gushed from the loud-speaker in a swirl of shadowed melody. Since Vienna died, all waltzes are shadowed.

The girl put her head on one side and hummed three or four bars and stopped with a sudden tightening of her mouth.

'Eve Cressy,' she said. 'It was in lights once. At a bum night club. A dive. They raided it and the lights went out.'

He smiled at her almost mockingly. 'It was no dive while you were there, Miss Cressy. . . . That's the waltz the orchestra always played when the old porter walked up and down in front of the hotel entrance, all swelled up with his medals on his chest. The Last Laugh. Emil Jannings. You wouldn't remember that one, Miss Cressy.'

'Spring, Beautiful Spring,' she said. 'No, I never saw it.'

He walked three steps away from her and turned. 'I have to go upstairs and palm door-knobs. I hope I didn't bother you. You ought to go to bed now. It's pretty late.'

The tinsel waltz stopped and a voice began to talk. The girl spoke through the voice. 'You really thought something like that – about the balcony?'

He nodded. 'I might have,' he said softly. 'I don't any more.'

'No chance, Tony.' Her smile was a dim lost leaf. 'Come and talk to me some more. Redheads don't jump, Tony. They hang on – and wither.'

He looked at her gravely for a moment and then moved away over the carpet. The porter was standing in the archway that led to the main lobby. Tony hadn't looked that way yet, but he knew somebody was there. He always knew if anybody was close to him. He could hear the grass grow like the donkey in The Blue Bird.

The porter jerked his chin at him urgently. His broad

face above the uniform collar looked sweaty and excited. Tony stepped up close to him and they went together through the arch and out to the middle of the dim lobby.

'Trouble?' Tony asked wearily.

'There's a guy outside to see you, Tony. He won't come in. I'm doing a wipe-off on the plate glass of the doors and he comes up beside me, a tall guy. "Get Tony," he says, out of the side of his mouth.'

Tony said: 'Uh-huh,' and looked at the porter's pale blue eyes. 'Who was it?'

'Al, he said to say it was.'

Tony's face became as expressionless as dough. 'Okay.' He started to move off.

The porter caught his sleeve. 'Listen, Tony. You got any enemies?'

Tony laughed politely, his face still like dough.

'Listen, Tony.' The porter held his sleeve tightly. 'There's a big black car down the block, the other way from the hacks. There's a guy standing beside it with his foot on the running board. This guy that spoke to me, he wears a dark-coloured, wrap-around overcoat with a high collar turned up against his ears. His hat's way low. You can't hardly see his face. He says, "Get Tony," out of the side of his mouth. You ain't got any enemies, have you, Tony?'

'Only the finance company,' Tony said. 'Beat it.'

He walked slowly and a little stiffly across the blue carpet, up the three shallow steps to the entrance lobby with the three elevators on one side and the desk on the other. Only one elevator was working. Beside the open doors, his arms folded, the night operator stood silent in a neat blue uniform with silver facings. A lean, dark Mexican named Gomez. A new boy, breaking in on the night shift.

The other side was the desk, rose marble, with the night clerk leaning on it delicately. A small neat man with a wispy reddish moustache and cheeks so rosy they looked rouged. He stared at Tony and poked a nail at his moustache.

Tony pointed a stiff index finger at him, folded the other three fingers tight to his palm, and flicked his thumb up and down on the stiff finger. The clerk touched the other side of his moustache and looked bored.

Tony went on past the closed and darkened news-stand and the side entrance to the drugstore, out to the brass-bound plate-glass doors. He stopped just inside them and took a deep, hard breath. He squared his shoulders, pushed the doors open and stepped out into the cold, damp night air.

The street was dark, silent. The rumble of traffic on Wilshire, two blocks away, had no body, no meaning. To the left were two taxis. Their drivers leaned against a fender, side by side, smoking. Tony walked the other way. The big dark car was a third of a block from the hotel entrance. Its lights were dimmed and it was only when he was almost up to it that he heard the gentle sound of its engine turning over.

A tall figure detached itself from the body of the car and strolled towards him, both hands in the pockets of the dark overcoat with the high collar. From the man's mouth a cigarette tip glowed faintly, a rusty pearl.

They stopped two feet from each other.

The tall man said: 'Hi, Tony. Long time no see.'

'Hello, Al. How's it going?'

'Can't complain.' The tall man started to take his right hand out of his overcoat pocket, then stopped and laughed quietly. 'I forgot. Guess you don't want to shake hands.'

'That don't mean anything,' Tony said. 'Shaking hands. Monkeys can shake hands. What's on your mind, Al?'

'Still the funny little fat guy, eh, Tony?'

'I guess.' Tony winked his eyes tight. His throat felt tight.

'You like your job back there?'

'It's a job.'

Al laughed his quiet laugh again. 'You take it slow, Tony. I'll take it fast. So it's a job and you want to hold it. Oke. There's a girl named Eve Cressy flopping in your quiet hotel. Get her out. Fast and right now.'

'What's the trouble?'

The tall man looked up and down the street. A man

behind in the car coughed lightly. 'She's hooked with a wrong number. Nothing against her personal, but she'll lead trouble to you. Get her out, Tony. You got maybe an hour.'

'Sure,' Tony said aimlessly, without meaning.

Al took his hand out of his pocket and stretched it against Tony's chest. He gave him a light, lazy push. 'I wouldn't be telling you just for the hell of it, little fat brother. Get her out of there.'

'Okay,' Tony said, without any tone in his voice.

The tall man took back his hand and reached for the car door. He opened it and started to slip in like a lean black shadow.

Then he stopped and said something to the men in the car and got out again. He came back to where Tony stood silent, his pale eyes catching a little dim light from the street.

'Listen, Tony. You always keep your nose clean. You're a good brother, Tony.'

Tony didn't speak.

Al leaned towards him, a long urgent shadow, the high collar almost touching his ears. 'It's trouble business, Tony. The boys won't like it, but I'm telling you just the same. This Cressy was married to a lad named Johnny Ralls. Ralls is out of Quentin two, three days, or a week. He did a three-spot for manslaughter. The girl put him there. He ran down an old man one night when he was drunk, and she was with him. He wouldn't stop. She told him to go in and tell it, or else. He didn't go in. So the Johns come for him.'

Tony said, 'That's too bad.'

'It's kosher, kid. It's my business to know. This Ralls flapped his mouth in stir about how the girl would be waiting for him when he got out, all set to forgive and forget, and he was going straight to her.'

Tony said: 'What's he to you?' His voice had a dry, stiff crackle, like thick paper.

Al laughed. 'The trouble boys want to see him. He ran a table at a spot on the Strip and figured out a scheme. He and another guy took the house for fifty grand. The other lad coughed up, but we still need Johnny's twenty-five. The trouble boys don't get paid to forget.'

Tony looked up and down the dark street. One of the taxi drivers flicked a cigarette stub in a long arc over the top of one of the cabs. Tony watched it fall and spark on the pavement. He listened to the quiet sound of the big car's motor.

'I don't want any part of it,' he said. 'I'll get her out.'

Al backed away from him, nodding. 'Wise kid. How's mom these days?'

'Okay,' Tony said.

'Tell her I was asking for her.'

'Asking for her isn't anything,' Tony said.

Al turned quickly and got into the car. The car curved lazily in the middle of the block and drifted back toward the corner. Its lights went up and sprayed on a wall. It turned a corner and was gone. The lingering smell of its exhaust drifted past Tony's nose. He turned and walked back to the hotel, and into it. He went along to the radio room.

The radio still muttered, but the girl was gone from the davenport in front of it. The pressed cushions were hollowed out by her body. Tony reached down and touched them. He thought they were still warm. He turned the radio off and stood there, turning a thumb slowly in front of his body, his hand flat against his stomach. Then he went back through the lobby toward the elevator bank and stood beside a majolica jar of white sand. The clerk fussed behind a pebbled-glass screen at one end of the desk. The air was dead.

The elevator bank was dark. Tony looked at the indicator of the middle car and saw that it was at 14.

'Gone to bed,' he said under his breath.

The door of the porter's room beside the elevators opened and the little Mexican night operator came out in street clothes. He looked at Tony with a quiet sidewise look out of eyes the colour of dried-out chestnuts.

'Good night, boss.'

'Yeah,' Tony said absently.

He took a thin dappled cigar out of his vest pocket and smelled it. He examined it slowly, turning it around in his neat fingers. There was a small tear along the side. He frowned at that and put the cigar away.

There was a distant sound and the hand on the indicator began to steal around the bronze dial. Light glittered up in the shaft and the straight line of the car floor dissolved the darkness below. The car stopped and the doors opened, and Carl came out of it.

His eyes caught Tony's with a kind of jump and he walked over to him, his head on one side, a thin shine along his pink upper lip.

'Listen, Tony.'

Tony took his arm in a hard swift hand and turned him. He pushed him quickly, yet somehow casually, down the steps to the dim main lobby and steered him into a corner. He let go of the arm. His throat tightened again, for no reason he could think of.

'Well?' he said darkly. 'Listen to what?'

The porter reached into a pocket and hauled out a dollar bill. 'He gimme this,' he said loosely. His glittering eyes looked past Tony's shoulder at nothing. They winked rapidly. 'Ice and ginger ale.'

'Don't stall,' Tony growled.

'Guy in 14B,' the porter said.

'Lemme smell your breath.'

The porter leaned towards him obediently.

'Liquor,' Tony said harshly.

'He gimme a drink.'

Tony looked down at the dollar bill. 'Nobody's in 14B. Not on my list,' he said.

'Yeah. There is.' The porter licked his lips, and his eyes opened and shut several times. 'Tall dark guy.'

'All right,' Tony said crossly. 'All right. There's a tall dark guy in 14B and he gave you a buck and a drink. Then what?'

'Gat under his arm,' Carl said, and blinked.

Tony smiled, but his eyes had taken on the lifeless glitter of thick ice. 'You take Miss Cressy up to her room?'

Carl shook his head. 'Gomez, I saw her go up.'

'Get away from me,' Tony said between his teeth. 'And don't accept any more drinks from the guests.'

He didn't move until Carl had gone back into his cubby-hole by the elevators and shut the door. Then he moved silently up the three steps and stood in front of the desk, looking at the veined rose marble, the onyx pen set, the fresh registration card in its leather frame. He lifted a hand and smacked it down hard on the marble. The clerk popped out from behind the glass screen like a chipmunk coming out of its hole.

Tony took a flimsy out of his breast pocket and spread it on the desk. 'No 14B on this,' he said in a bitter voice.

The clerk wiped politely at his moustache. 'So sorry. You must have been out to supper when he checked in.'

'Who?'

'Registered as James Watterson, San Diego.' The clerk yawned.

'Ask for anybody?'

The clerk stopped in the middle of the yawn and looked at the top of Tony's head. 'Why, yes. He asked for a swing band. Why?'

'Smart, fast, and funny,' Tony said. 'If you like 'em that way.' He wrote on his flimsy and stuffed it back into his pocket. 'I'm going upstairs and palm doorknobs. There's four tower rooms you ain't rented yet. Get up on your toes, son. You're slipping.'

'I make out,' the clerk drawled, and completed his yawn. 'Hurry back, pop. I don't know how I'll get through the time.'

'You could shave that pink fuzz off your lip,' Tony said, and went across to the elevators.

He opened up a dark one and lit the dome light and shot the car up to fourteen. He darkened it again, stepped out and closed the doors. This lobby was smaller than any other, except the one immediately below it. It had a single blue-panelled door in each of the walls other than the elevator wall. On each door was a gold number and letter with a gold wreath around it. Tony walked over to 14A and put his ear to the panel. He heard nothing. Eve Cressy might be in bed asleep, or in the bathroom, or out on the balcony. Or she might be sitting there in the room, a few feet from the door, looking at the wall. Well, he wouldn't expect to be able to hear her sit and look at the wall. He went over to 14B and put his ear to that panel. This was different. There was a sound in there. A man coughed. It sounded somehow like a solitary cough. There were no voices. Tony pressed the small nacre button beside the door.

Steps came without hurry. A thickened voice spoke through the panel. Tony made no answer, no sound. The thickened voice repeated the question. Lightly, maliciously, Tony pressed the bell again.

Mr James Watterson, of San Diego, should now open the door and give forth noise. He didn't. A silence fell beyond that door that was like the silence of a glacier. Once more Tony put his ear to the wood. Silence utterly.

He got out a master key on a chain and pushed it delicately into the lock of the door. He turned it, pushed the door inward three inches, and withdrew the key. Then he waited.

'All right,' the voice said harshly. 'Come in and get it.'

Tony pushed the door wide open and stood there, framed against the light from the lobby. The man was tall, black-haired, angular, and white-faced. He held a gun. He held it as though he knew about guns.

'Step right in,' he drawled.

Tony went in through the door and pushed it shut with his shoulder. He kept his hands a little out from his sides, the clever fingers curled and slack. He smiled his quiet little smile.

'Mr Watterson?'

'And after that what?'

'I'm the house detective here.'

'It slays me.'

The tall, white-faced, somehow handsome and somehow not handsome man backed slowly into the room. It was a large room with a low balcony around two sides of it. French doors opened out on the little, private, open-air balcony that each of the tower rooms had. There was a grate set for a log fire behind a panelled screen in front of a cheerful davenport. A tall misted glass stood on a hotel tray beside a deep, cosy chair. The man backed toward this and stood in front of it. The large glistening gun drooped and pointed at the floor.

'It slays me,' he said. 'I'm in the dump an hour and the house copper gives me the buzz. Okay, sweetheart, look in the closet and bathroom. But she just left.'

'You didn't see her yet,' Tony said.

The man's bleached face filled with unexpected lines.

His thickened voice edged toward a snarl. 'Yeah? Who didn't I see yet?'

'A girl named Eve Cressy.'

The man swallowed. He put his gun down on the table beside the tray. He let himself down into the chair backwards, stiffly, like a man with a touch of lumbago. Then he leaned forward and put his hands on his kneecaps and smiled brightly between his teeth. 'So she got here, huh? I didn't ask about her yet. I'm a careful guy. I didn't ask yet.'

'She's been here five days,' Tony said. 'Waiting for you. She hasn't left the hotel a minute.'

The man's mouth worked a little. His smile had a knowing tilt to it. 'I got delayed a little up north,' he said smoothly. 'You know how it is. Visiting old friends. You seem to know a lot about my business, copper.'

'That's right, Mr Ralls.'

The man lunged to his feet and his hand snapped at the gun. He stood leaning over, holding it on the table, staring. 'Dames talk too much,' he said with a muffled sound in his voice, as though he held something soft between his teeth and talked through it.

'Not dames, Mr Ralls.'

'Huh?' The gun slithered on the hard wood of the table. 'Talk it up, copper. My mind reader just quit.'

'Not dames, Guys. Guys with guns.'

The glacier silence fell between them again. The man straightened his body slowly. His face was washed clean of expression, but his eyes were haunted. Tony leaned in front of him, a shortish plump man with a quiet, pale, friendly face and eyes as simple as forest water.

'They never run out of gas – those boys,' Johnny Ralls said, and licked at his lip. 'Early and late, they work. The old firm never sleeps.'

'You know who they are?' Tony said softly.

'I could maybe give nine guesses. And twelve of them would be right.'

'The trouble boys,' Tony said, and smiled a brittle smile.

'Where is she?' Johnny Ralls asked harshly.

'Right next door to you.'

The man walked to the wall and left his gun lying

on the table. He stood in front of the wall, studying it. He reached up and gripped the grillwork of the balcony railing. When he dropped his hand and turned, his face had lost some of its lines. His eyes had a quieter glint. He moved back to Tony and stood over him.

'I've got a stake,' he said. 'Eve sent me some dough and I built it up with a touch I made up north. Case dough, what I mean. The trouble boys talk about twenty-five grand.' He smiled crookedly. 'Five C's I can count. I'd have a lot of fun making them believe that, I would.'

'What did you do with it?' Tony asked indifferently.

'I never had it, copper. Leave that lay. I'm the only guy in the world that believes it. It was a little deal I got suckered on.'

'I'll believe it,' Tony said.

'They don't kill often. But they can be awful tough.'

'Mugs,' Tony said with a sudden bitter contempt. 'Guys with guns. Just mugs.'

Johnny Ralls reached for his glass and drained it empty. The ice cubes tinkled softly as he put it down. He picked his gun up, danced it on his palm, then tucked it, nose down, into an inner breast pocket. He stared at the carpet.

'How come you're telling me this, copper?'

'I thought maybe you'd give her a break.'

'And if I wouldn't?'

'I kind of think you will,' Tony said.

Johnny Ralls nodded quietly. 'Can I get out of here?'

'You could take the service elevator to the garage. You could rent a car. I can give you a card to the garageman.'

'You're a funny little guy,' Johnny Ralls said.

Tony took out a worn ostrich-skin billfold and scribbled on a printed card. Johnny Ralls read it, and stood holding it, tapping it against a thumbnail.

'I could take her with me,' he said, his eyes narrow.

'You could take a ride in a basket too,' Tony said. 'She's been here five days, I told you. She's been spotted. A guy I know called me up and told me to get her out of here. Told me what it was all about. So I'm getting you out instead.'

'They'll love that,' Johnny Ralls said. 'They'll send you violets.'

'I'll weep about it on my day off.'

Johnny Ralls turned his hand over and stared at the palm. 'I could see her, anyway. Before I blow. Next door to here, you said?'

Tony turned on his heel and started for the door. He said over his shoulder, 'Don't waste a lot of time, handsome. I might change my mind.'

The man said, almost gently: 'You might be spotting me right now, for all I know.'

Tony didn't turn his head. 'That's a chance you have to take.'

He went on to the door and passed out of the room. He shut it carefully, silently, looked once at the door of 14A and got into his dark elevator. He rode it down to the linen-room floor and got out to remove the basket that held the service elevator open at that floor. The door slid quietly shut. He held it so that it made no noise. Down the corridor, light came from the open door of the housekeeper's office. Tony got back into his elevator and went on down to the lobby.

The little clerk was out of sight behind his pebbled-glass screen, auditing accounts. Tony went through the main lobby and turned into the radio room. The radio was on again, soft. She was there, curled on the davenport again. The speaker hummed to her, a vague sound so low that what it said was as wordless as the murmur of trees. She turned her head slowly and smiled at him.

'Finished palming doorknobs? I couldn't sleep worth a nickel. So I came down again. Okay?'

He smiled and nodded. He sat down in a green chair and patted the plump brocade arms of it. 'Sure, Miss Cressy.'

'Waiting is the hardest kind of work, isn't it? I wish you'd talk to that radio. It sounds like a pretzel being bent.'

Tony fiddled with it, got nothing he liked, set it back where it had been.

'Beer-parlour drunks are all the customers now.'

She smiled at him again.

'I don't bother you being here, Miss Cressy?'

'I like it. You're a sweet little guy, Tony.'

He looked stiffly at the floor and a ripple touched his spine. He waited for it to go away. It went slowly. Then he sat back, relaxed again, his neat fingers clasped on his elk's tooth. He listened. Not to the radio – to far-off, uncertain things, menacing things. And perhaps to just the safe whirr of wheels going away into a strange night.

'Nobody's all bad,' he said out loud.

The girl looked at him lazily. 'I've met two or three I was wrong on, then.'

He nodded. 'Yeah,' he admitted judiciously. 'I guess there's some that are.'

The girl yawned and her deep violet eyes half closed. She nestled back into the cushions. 'Sit there a while, Tony. Maybe I could nap.'

'Sure. Not a thing for me to do. Don't know why they pay me.'

She slept quickly and with complete stillness, like a child. Tony hardly breathed for ten minutes. He just watched her, his mouth a little open. There was a quiet fascination in his limpid eyes, as if he was looking at an altar.

Then he stood up with infinite care and padded away under the arch to the entrance lobby and the desk. He stood at the desk for a little while. He heard a pen rustling out of sight. He went around the corner to the row of house phones in little glass cubbyholes. He lifted one and asked the night operator for the garage.

It rang three or four times and then a boyish voice answered: 'Windermere Hotel. Garage speaking.'

'This is Tony Reseck. That guy Watterson I gave a card to. He leave?'

'Sure, Tony. Half an hour almost. Is it your charge?'

'Yeah,' Tony said. 'My party. Thanks. Be seein' you.'

He hung up and scratched his neck. He went back to the desk and slapped a hand on it. The clerk wafted himself around the screen with his greeter's smile in place. It dropped when he saw Tony.

'Can't a guy catch up on his work?' he grumbled.

'What's the professional rate on 14B?'

The clerk stared morosely. 'There's no professional rate in the tower.'

'Make one. The fellow left already. Was there only an hour.'

'Well, well,' the clerk said airily. 'So the personality didn't click to-night. We get a skip-out.'

'Will five bucks satisfy you?'

'Friend of yours?'

'No. Just a drunk with delusions of grandeur and no dough.'

'Guess we'll have to let it ride, Tony. How did he get out?'

'I took him down the service elevator. You was asleep. Will five bucks satisfy you?'

'Why?'

The worn ostrich-skin wallet came out and a weedy five slipped across the marble. 'All I could shake him for,' Tony said loosely.

The clerk took the five and looked puzzled. 'You're the boss,' he said, and shrugged. The phone shrilled on the desk and he reached for it. He listened and then pushed it toward Tony. 'For you.'

Tony took the phone and cuddled it close to his chest. He put his mouth close to the transmitter. The voice was strange to him. It had a metallic sound. Its syllables were meticulously anonymous.

'Tony? Tony Reseck?'

'Talking.'

'A message from Al. Shoot?'

Tony looked at the clerk. 'Be a pal,' he said over the mouthpiece. The clerk flicked a narrow smile at him and went away. 'Shoot,' Tony said into the phone.

'We had a little business with a guy in your place. Picked him up scramming. Al had a hunch you'd run him out. Tailed him and took him to the kerb. Not so good. Backfire.'

Tony held the phone very tight and his temples chilled with the evaporation of moisture. 'Go on,' he said. 'I guess there's more.'

'A little. The guy stopped the big one. Cold. Al – Al said to tell you good-bye.'

Tony leaned hard against the desk. His mouth made a sound that was not speech.

'Get it?' The metallic voice sounded impatient, a little bored. 'This guy had him a rod. He used it. Al won't be phoning anybody any more.'

Tony lurched at the phone, and the base of it shook on the rose marble. His mouth was a hard dry knot.

The voice said: 'That's as far as we go, bud. G'night.' The phone clicked dryly, like a pebble hitting a wall.

Tony put the phone down in its cradle very carefully, so as not to make any sound. He looked at the clenched palm of his left hand. He took a handkerchief out and rubbed the palm softly and straightened his fingers out with his other hand. Then he wiped his forehead. The clerk came around the screen again and looked at him with glinting eyes.

'I'm off Friday. How about lending me that phone number?'

Tony nodded at the clerk and smiled a minute frail smile. He put his handkerchief away and patted the pocket he had put it in. He turned and walked away from the desk, across the entrance lobby, down the three shallow steps, along the shadowy reaches of the main lobby, and so in through the arch to the radio room once more. He walked softly, like a man moving in a room where somebody is very sick. He reached the chair he had sat in before and lowered himself into it inch by inch. The girl slept on, motionless, in that curled-up looseness achieved by some women and all cats. Her breath made not the slightest sound against the vague murmur of the radio.

Tony Reseck leaned back in the chair and clasped his hands on his elk's tooth and quietly closed his eyes.

The Snatching of Bookie Bob

Damon Runyon

Now it comes on the spring of 1931, after a long hard winter, and times are very tough indeed, what with the stock market going all to pieces, and banks busting right and left, and the law getting very nasty about this and that, and one thing and another, and many citizens of this town are compelled to do the best they can.

There is very little scratch anywhere and along Broadway many citizens are wearing their last year's clothes and have practically nothing to bet on the races or anything else, and it is a condition that will touch anybody's heart.

So I am not surprised to hear rumours that the snatching of certain parties is going on in spots, because while snatching is by no means a high-class business, and is even considered somewhat illegal, it is something to tide over the hard times.

Furthermore, I am not surprised to hear that this snatching is being done by a character by the name of Harry the Horse, who comes from Brooklyn, and who is a character who does not care much what sort of business he is in, and who is mobbed up with other characters from Brooklyn such as Spanish John and Little Isadore, who do not care what sort of business they are in, either.

In fact, Harry the Horse and Spanish John and Little Isadore are very hard characters in every respect, and there is considerable indignation expressed around and about when they move over from Brooklyn into Manhattan and start snatching, because the citizens of Manhattan feel that if there is any snatching done in their territory, they are entitled to do it themselves.

But Harry the Horse and Spanish John and Little Isadore pay no attention whatever to local sentiment and go on the snatch on a pretty fair scale, and by and by I am hearing rumours of some very nice scores. These scores are not extra large scores, to be sure, but they are enough to keep the wolf from the door, and in fact from three different doors, and before long Harry the Horse and Spanish John and Little Isadore are around the race-tracks betting on the horses, because if there is one thing they are all very proud of, it is betting on the horses.

Now many citizens have the wrong idea entirely of the snatching business. Many citizens think that all there is to snatching is to round up the party who is to be snatched and then just snatch him, putting him away somewhere until his family or friends dig up enough scratch to pay whatever price the snatchers are asking. Very few citizens understand that the snatching business must be well organized and very systematic.

In the first place, if you are going to do any snatching, you cannot snatch just anybody. You must know who you are snatching, because naturally it is no good snatching somebody who does not have any scratch to settle with. And you cannot tell by the way a party looks or how he lives in this town if he has any scratch, because many a party who is around in automobiles, and wearing good clothes, and chucking quite a swell is nothing but the phonus bolonus and does not have any real scratch whatever.

So of course such a party is no good for snatching, and of course guys who are on the snatch cannot go around inquiring into bank accounts, or asking how much this and that party has in a safe-deposit vault, because such questions are apt to make citizens wonder why, and it is very dangerous to get citizens to wondering why about anything. So the only way guys who are on the snatch can find out about parties worth snatching is to make a connection with some guy who can put the finger on the right party.

The finger guy must know the party he fingers has plenty of ready scratch to begin with, and he must also know that this party is such a party as is not apt to make too much disturbance about being snatched, such as telling the gendarmes. The party may be a legitimate party, such as a business guy, but he will have reasons why he does not wish it to get out that he is snatched, and the finger must know these reasons. Maybe the party is not leading the right sort of life, such as running around with blondes when he has an ever-loving wife and seven children in Mamaroneck, but does not care to have his habits known, as is apt to happen if he is snatched, especially if he is snatched when he is with a blonde.

And sometimes the party is such a party as does not care to have matches run up and down the bottom of his feet, which often happens to parties who are snatched and who do not seem to wish to settle their bill promptly, because many parties are very ticklish on the bottom of the feet, especially if the matches are lit. On the other hand, maybe the party is not a legitimate guy, such as a party who is running a crap game or a swell speakeasy, or who has some other dodge he does not care to have come out, and who also does not care about having his feet tickled.

Such a party is very good indeed for the snatching business, because he is pretty apt to settle without any argument. And after a party settles one snatching, it will be considered very unethical for anybody else to snatch him again very soon, so he is not likely to make any fuss about the matter. The finger guy gets a commission of twenty-five per cent of the settlement, and one and all are satisfied and much fresh scratch comes into circulation, which is very good for the merchants. And while the party who is snatched may know who snatches him, one thing he never knows is who puts the finger on him, this being considered a trade secret.

I am talking to Waldo Winchester, the newspaper scribe, one night and something about the snatching business comes up, and Waldo Winchester is trying to tell me that it is one of the oldest dodges in the world, only Waldo calls it kidnapping, which is a title that will be very repulsive to guys who are on the snatch nowadays. Waldo Winchester claims that hundreds of years ago guys are around snatching parties, male and female, and holding them for ransom, and furthermore Waldo Winchester says that they even snatch very little children and Waldo states that it is all a very, very wicked proposition.

Well, I can see where Waldo is right about it being wicked to snatch dolls and little children, but of course no guys who are on the snatch nowadays will ever think of such a thing, because who is going to settle for a doll in these times when you can scarcely even give them away? As for little children, they are apt to be a great nuisance, because their mammas are sure to go running around hollering bloody murder about them, and furthermore little children are very dangerous, indeed, what with being apt to break out with measles and mumps and one thing and another any minute and give it to everybody in the neighbourhood.

Well, anyway, knowing that Harry the Horse and Spanish John and Little Isadore are now on the snatch, I am by no means pleased to see them coming along one Tuesday evening when I am standing at the corner of Fiftieth and Broadway, although of course I give them a very jolly hello, and say I hope and trust they are feeling nicely.

They stand there talking to me a few minutes, and I am very glad indeed that Johnny Brannigan, the strong-arm cop, does not happen along and see us, because it will give Johnny a very bad impression of me to see me in such company, even though I am not responsible for the company. But naturally I cannot haul off and walk away from this company at once, because Harry the Horse and Spanish Joe and Little Isadore may get the idea that I am playing the chill for them, and will feel hurt.

'Well,' I say to Harry the Horse, 'how are things going, Harry?'

'They are going no good,' Harry says. 'We do not beat a race in four days. In fact,' he says, 'we go overboard to-day. We are washed out. We owe every bookmaker at the track that will trust us, and now we are out trying to raise some scratch to pay off. A guy must pay his bookmaker no matter what.'

Well, of course this is very true, indeed, because if a

guy does not pay his bookmaker it will lower his business standing quite some, as the bookmaker is sure to go around putting the blast on him, so I am pleased to hear Harry the Horse mention such honourable principles.

'By the way,' Harry says, 'do you know a guy by the name of Bookie Bob?'

Now I do not know Bookie Bob personally, but of course I know who Bookie Bob is, and so does everybody else in this town that ever goes to a race-track, because Bookie Bob is the biggest bookmaker around and about, and has plenty of scratch. Furthermore, it is the opinion of one and all that Bookie Bob will die with this scratch, because he is considered a very close guy with his scratch. In fact, Bookie Bob is considered closer than a dead heat.

He is a short fat guy with a bald head, and his head is always shaking a little from side to side, which some say is a touch of palsy, but which most citizens believe comes of Bookie Bob shaking his head 'No' to guys asking for credit in betting on the races. He has an ever-loving wife, who is a very quiet little old doll with grey hair and a very sad look in her eyes, but nobody can blame her for this when they figure that she lives with Bookie Bob for many years.

I often see Bookie Bob and his ever-loving wife eating in different joints along in the Forties, because they seem to have no home except an hotel, and many a time I hear Bookie Bob giving her a going-over about something or other, and generally it is about the price of something she orders to eat, so I judge Bookie Bob is as tough with his ever-loving wife about scratch as he is with everybody else. In fact, I hear him bawling her out one night because she has on a new hat which she says cost her six bucks, and Bookie Bob wishes to know if she is trying to ruin him with her extravagances.

But of course I am not criticizing Bookie Bob for squawking about the hat, because for all I know six bucks may be too much for a doll to pay for a hat, at that. And furthermore, maybe Bookie Bob has the right idea about keeping down his ever-loving wife's appetite, because I know many a guy in this town who is practically ruined by dolls eating too much on him.

'Well,' I say to Harry the Horse, 'if Bookie Bob is one of the bookmakers you owe, I am greatly surprised to see that you seem to have both eyes in your head, because I never before hear of Bookie Bob letting anybody owe him without giving him at least one of their eyes for security. In fact,' I say, 'Bookie Bob is such a guy as will not give you the right time if he has two watches.'

'No,' Harry the Horse says, 'we do not owe Bookie Bob. But,' he says, 'he will be owing us before long. We are going to put the snatch on Bookie Bob.'

Well, this is most disquieting news to me, not because I care if they snatch Bookie Bob or not, but because somebody may see me talking to them who will remember about it when Bookie Bob is snatched. But of course it will not be good policy for me to show Harry the Horse and Spanish John and Little Isadore that I am nervous, so I only speak as follows:

'Harry,' I say, 'every man knows his own business best, and I judge you know what you are doing. But,' I say, 'you are snatching a hard guy when you snatch Bookie Bob. A very hard guy, indeed. In fact,' I say, 'I hear the softest thing about him is his front teeth, so it may be very difficult for you to get him to settle after you snatch him.'

'No,' Harry the Horse says, 'we will have no trouble about it. Our finger gives us Bookie Bob's hole card, and it is a most surprising thing, indeed. But,' Harry the Horse says, 'you come upon many surprising things in human nature when you are on the snatch. Bookie Bob's hole card is his ever-loving wife's opinion of him.

'You see,' Harry the Horse says, 'Bookie Bob has been putting himself away with his ever-loving wife for years as a very important guy in this town, with much power and influence, although of course Bookie Bob knows very well he stands about as good as a broken leg. In fact,' Harry the Horse says, 'Bookie Bob figures that his ever-loving wife is the only one in the world who looks on him as a big guy, and he will sacrifice even his scratch, or anyway some of it, rather than let her know that guys have such little respect for him as to put the snatch on him. It is what you call psychology.' Harry the Horse says.

Well, this does not make good sense to me, and I am thinking to myself that the psychology that Harry the Horse really figures to work out nice on Bookie Bob is tickling his feet with matches, but I am not anxious to stand there arguing about it, and pretty soon I bid them all good evening, very polite, and take the wind, and I do not see Harry the Horse or Spanish John or Little Isadore again for a month.

In the meantime, I hear gossip here and there that Bookie Bob is missing for several days, and when he finally shows up again he gives it out that he is very sick during his absence, but I can put two and two together as well as anybody in this town and I figure that Bookie Bob is snatched by Harry the Horse and Spanish John and Little Isadore, and the chances are it costs him plenty.

So I am looking for Harry the Horse and Spanish John and Little Isadore to be around the race-track with plenty of scratch and betting them higher than a cat's back, but they never show up, and what is more I hear they leave Manhattan, and are back in Brooklyn working every day handling beer. Naturally this is very surprising to me, because the way things are running beer is a tough dodge just now, and there is very little profit in same, and I figure that with the scratch they must make off Bookie Bob, Harry the Horse and Spanish John and Little Isadore have a right to be taking things easy.

Now one night I am in Good Time Charley Bernstein's little speak in Forty-eighth Street, talking of this and that with Charley, when in comes Harry the Horse, looking very weary and by no means prosperous. Naturally I gave him a large hello, and by and by we get to gabbing together and I ask him whatever becomes of the Bookie Bob matter, and Harry the Horse tells me as follows:

Yes [Harry the Horse says], we snatch Bookie Bob all right. In fact, we snatch him the very next night after we are talking to you, or on a Wednesday night. Our finger tells us Bookie Bob is going to a wake over in his old neighbourhood on Tenth Avenue, near Thirty-eighth Street, and this is where we pick him up.

He is leaving the place in his car along about midnight, and of course Bookie Bob is alone as he seldom lets anybody ride with him because of the wear and tear on his car cushions, and Little Isadore swings our flivver in front of him and makes him stop. Naturally Bookie Bob is greatly surprised when I poke my head into his car and tell him I wish the pleasure of his company for a short time, and at first he is inclined to argue the matter, saying I must make a mistake, but I put the old convincer on him by letting him peek down the snozzle of my John Roscoe.

We lock his car and throw the keys away, and then we take Bookie Bob in our car and go to a certain spot on Eighth Avenue where we have a nice little apartment all ready. When we get there I tell Bookie Bob that he can call up anybody he wishes and state that the snatch is on him and that it will require twenty-five G's, cash money, to take it off, but of course I also tell Bookie Bob that he is not to mention where he is or something may happen to him.

Well, I will say one thing for Bookie Bob, although everybody is always weighing in the sacks on him and saying he is not good – he takes it like a gentleman, and very calm and businesslike.

Furthermore, he does not seem alarmed, as many citizens are when they find themselves in such a situation. He recognizes the justice of our claim at once, saying as follows:

'I will telephone my partner, Sam Salt,' he says. 'He is the only one I can think of who is apt to have such a sum as twenty-five G's cash money. But,' he says, 'if you gentlemen will pardon the question, because this is a new experience to me, how do I know everything will be okay for me after you get the scratch?'

'Why,' I say to Bookie Bob, somewhat indignant, 'it is well known to one and all in this town that my word is my bond. There are two things I am bound to do,' I say, 'and one is to keep my word in such a situation as this, and the other is to pay anything I owe a bookmaker, no matter what, for these are obligations of honour to me.'

'Well,' Bookie Bob says, 'of course I do not know you gentlemen, and, in fact, I do not remember seeing any of you, although your face is somewhat familiar, but if you pay your bookmaker you are an honest guy, and one in a million. In fact,' Bookie Bob says, 'if I have all the scratch that is owing to me around this town, I will not be telephoning anybody for such a sum as twenty-five G's. I will have such a sum in my pants pocket for change.'

Now Bookie Bob calls a certain number and talks to somebody there but he does not get Sam Salt, and he seems much disappointed when he hangs up the receiver again.

'This is a very tough break for me,' he says. 'Sam Salt goes to Atlantic City an hour ago on very important business and will not be back until to-morrow evening, and they do not know where he is to stay in Atlantic City. And,' Bookie Bob says, 'I cannot think of anybody else to call up to get this scratch, especially anybody I will care to have know I am in this situation.'

'Why not call your ever-loving wife?' I say. 'Maybe she can dig up this kind of scratch.'

'Say,' Bookie Bob says, 'you do not suppose I am chump enough to give my ever-loving wife twenty-five G's, or even let her know where she can get her dukes on twenty-five G's belonging to me, do you? I give my ever-loving wife ten bucks per week for spending money,' Bookie Bob says, 'and this is enough scratch for any doll, especially when you figure I pay for her meals.'

Well, there seems to be nothing we can do except wait until Sam Salt gets back, but we let Bookie Bob call his ever-loving wife, as Bookie Bob says he does not wish to have her worrying about his absence, and tells her a big lie about having to go to Jersey City to sit up with a sick Brother Elk.

Well, it is now nearly four o'clock in the morning, so we put Bookie Bob in a room with Little Isadore to sleep, although, personally, I consider making a guy sleep with Little Isadore very cruel treatment, and Spanish John and I take turns keeping awake and watching out that Bookie Bob does not take the air on us before paying us off. To tell the truth, Little Isadore and Spanish John are somewhat disappointed that Bookie Bob agrees to settle so promptly, because they are looking forward to tickling his feet with great relish.

Now Bookie Bob turns out to be very good company when he wakes up the next morning, because he knows a lot of race-track stories and plenty of scandal, and he keeps us much interested at breakfast. He talks along with us as if he knows us all his life, and he seems very nonchalant indeed, but the chances are he will not be so nonchalant if I tell him about Spanish John's thought.

Well, about noon Spanish John goes out of the apartment and comes back with a racing sheet, because he knows Little Isadore and I will be wishing to know what is running in different spots although we do not have anything to bet on these races, or any way of betting on them, because we are overboard with every bookmaker we know.

Now Bookie Bob is also much interested in the matter of what is running, especially at Belmont, and he is bending over the table with me and Spanish John and Little Isadore, looking at the sheet, when Spanish John speaks as follows:

'My goodness,' Spanish John says, 'a spot such as this fifth race with Questionnaire at four to five is like finding money in the street. I only wish I have a few bobs to bet on him at such a price,' Spanish John says.

'Why,' Bookie Bob says, very polite, 'if you gentlemen wish to bet on these races I will gladly book to you. It is a good way to pass away the time while we are waiting for Sam Salt, unless you will rather play pinochle?'

'But,' I say, 'we have no scratch to play the races, at least not much.'

'Well,' Bookie Bob says, 'I will take your markers, because I hear what you say about always paying your bookmaker, and you put yourself away with me as an honest guy, and these other gentlemen also impress me as honest guys.'

Now what happens but we begin betting Bookie Bob on the different races, not only at Belmont, but at all the other tracks in the country, for Little Isadore and

Spanish John and I are guys who like plenty of action when we start betting on the horses. We write out markers for whatever we wish to bet and hand them to Bookie Bob, and Bookie Bob sticks these markers in an inside pocket, and along in the late afternoon it looks as if he has a tumour on his chest.

We get the race results by phone off a poolroom downtown as fast as they come off, and also the prices, and it is a lot of fun, and Little Isadore and Spanish John and Bookie Bob and I are all little pals together until all the races are over and Bookie Bob takes out the markers and starts counting himself up.

It comes out then that I owe Bookie Bob ten G's, and Spanish John owes him six G's, and Little Isadore owes him four G's, as Little Isadore beats him a couple of races out west.

Well, about this time, Bookie Bob manages to get Sam Salt on the phone, and explains to Sam that he is to go to a certain safe-deposit box and get out twenty-five G's, and then wait until midnight and hire himself a taxicab and start riding around the block between Fifty-first and Fifty-second, from Eighth to Ninth avenues, and to keep riding until somebody flags the cab and takes the scratch off him.

Naturally Sam Salt understands right away that the snatch is on Bookie Bob, and he agrees to do as he is told, but he says he cannot do it until the following night because he knows there is not twenty-five G's in the box, and he will have to get the difference at the track the next day. So there we are with another day in the apartment and Spanish John and Little Isadore and I are just as well pleased because Bookie Bob has us hooked and we naturally wish to wiggle off.

But the next day is worse than ever. In all the years I am playing the horses I never have such a tough day, and Spanish John and Little Isadore are just as bad. In fact, we are all going so bad that Bookie Bob begins to feel sorry for us and often lays us a couple of points above the track prices, but it does no good. At the end of the day, I am in a total of twenty G's, while Spanish John owes fifteen, and Little Isadore fifteen, a total of fifty G's among the three of us. But we are never any hands to hold post-mortems on bad days, so Little Isadore goes out to a delicatessen store and lugs in a lot of nice things to eat, and we have a fine dinner, and then we sit around with Bookie Bob telling stories, and even singing a few songs together until time to meet Sam Salt.

When it comes on midnight Spanish John goes out and lays for Sam, and gets a little valise off of Sam Salt. Then Spanish John comes back to the apartment and we open the valise and the twenty-five G's are there okay, and we cut this scratch three ways.

Then I tell Bookie Bob he is free to go on about his business, and good luck to him, at that, but Bookie Bob looks at me as if he is very much surprised, and hurt, and says to me like this:

'Well, gentlemen, thank you for your courtesy, but what about the scratch you owe me? What about those markers? Surely, gentlemen, you will pay your bookmaker?'

Well, of course we owe Bookie Bob these markers, all right, and of course a man must pay his bookmaker, no matter what, so I hand over my bit and Bookie Bob puts down something in a little note-book that he takes out of his kick.

Then Spanish John and Little Isadore hand over their dough, too, and Bookie Bob puts down something more in the little note-book.

'Now,' Bookie Bob says, 'I credit each of your accounts with these payments, but you gentlemen still owe me a matter of twenty-five G's over and above the twenty-five I credit you with, and I hope and trust you will make arrangements to settle this at once because,' he says, 'I do not care to extend such accommodations over any considerable period.'

'But,' I say, 'we do not have any more scratch after paying you the twenty-five G's on account.'

'Listen,' Bookie Bob says, dropping his voice down to a whisper, 'what about putting the snatch on my partner, Sam Salt, and I will wait over a couple of days with you and keep booking to you, and maybe you can pull yourselves out. But of course,' Bookie Bob whispers, 'I will be entitled to twenty-five per cent of the snatch for putting the finger on Sam for you.'

But Spanish John and Little Isadore are sick and tired of Bookie Bob and will not listen to staying in the apartment any longer, because they say he is a jinx to them and they cannot beat him in any manner, shape, or form. Furthermore, I am personally anxious to get away because something Bookie Bob says reminds me of something.

It reminds me that besides the scratch we owe him, we forget to take out six G's two-fifty for the party who puts the finger on Bookie Bob for us, and this is a very serious matter indeed, because anybody will tell you that failing to pay a finger is considered a very dirty trick. Furthermore, if it gets around that you fail to pay a finger, nobody else will ever finger for you.

So [Harry the Horse says] we quit the snatching business because there is no use continuing while this obligation is outstanding against us, and we go back to Brooklyn to earn enough scratch to pay our just debts.

We are paying off Bookie Bob's IOU a little at a time, because we do not wish to ever have anybody say we welsh on a bookmaker, and furthermore we are paying off the six G's two-fifty commission we owe our finger.

And while it is tough going, I am glad to say our honest effort is doing somebody a little good, because I see Bookie Bob's ever-loving wife the other night all dressed up in new clothes and looking very happy, indeed.

And while a guy is telling me she is looking so happy because she gets a large legacy from an uncle who dies in Switzerland, and is now independent of Bookie Bob, I can only hope and trust [Harry the Horse says] that it never gets out that our finger in this case is nobody but Bookie Bob's ever-loving wife.

The Day of the Bullet

Stanley Ellin

I believe that in each lifetime there is one day of destiny. It may be a day chosen by the Fates who sit clucking and crooning over a spinning wheel, or, perhaps, by the gods whose mill grinds slow, but grinds exceedingly fine. It may be a day of sunshine or rain, of heat or cold. It is probably a day which none of us is aware of at the time, or can even recall through hindsight.

But for every one of us there is that day. And when it leads to a bad end it's better not to look back and search it out. What you discover may hurt, and it's a futile hurt because nothing can be done about it any longer. Nothing at all.

I realize that there is a certain illogic in believing this, something almost mystical. Certainly it would win the ready disfavour of those modern exorcists and dabblers with crystal balls, those psychologists and sociologists and case workers who – using their own peculiar language to express it – believe that there may be a way of controlling the fantastic conjunction of time, place, and event that we must all meet at some invisible crossroads on the Day. But they are wrong. Like the rest of us they can only be wise after the event.

In this case – and the word 'case' is particularly fitting here – the event was the murder of a man I had not seen for thirty-five years. Not since a summer day in 1923, or, to be even more exact, the evening of a summer day in 1923 when as boys we faced each other on a street in Brooklyn, and then went our ways, never to meet again.

We were only twelve years old then, he and I, but I remember the date because the next day my family moved to Manhattan, an earth-shaking event in itself.

And with dreadful clarity I remember the scene when we parted, and the last thing said there. I understand it now, and know it was the boy's day. The Day of the Bullet it might be called – although the bullet itself was not to be fired until thirty-five years later.

I learned about the murder from the front page of the newspaper my wife was reading at the breakfast table. She held the paper upright and partly folded, but the fold could not conceal from me the unappetizing picture on the front page, the photograph of a man slumped behind the wheel of his car, head clotted with blood, eyes staring and mouth gaping in the throes of violent and horrifying death.

The picture meant nothing to me, any more than did its shouting headline – RACKETS BOSS SHOT TO DEATH. All I thought, in fact, was that there were pleasanter objects to stare at over one's coffee and toast.

Then my eye fell on the caption below the picture, and I almost dropped my cup of coffee. *The body of Ignace Kovac*, said the caption, *Brooklyn racket boss who last night –*

I took the paper from my wife's hand while she looked at me in astonishment, and studied the picture closely. There was no question about it. I had not seen Ignace Kovac since we were kids together, but I could not mistake him, even in the guise of this dead and bloody hulk. And the most terrible part of it, perhaps, was that next to him, resting against the seat of the car, was a bag of golf clubs. Those golf clubs were all my memory needed to work on.

I was called back to the present by my wife's voice. 'Well,' she said with good-natured annoyance, 'considering that I'm right in the middle of Walter Winchell –'

I returned the paper to her. 'I'm sorry. I got a jolt when I saw that picture. I used to know him.'

Her eyes lit up with the interest of one who – even at secondhand – finds herself in the presence of the notorious. 'You did? When?'

'Oh, when the folks still lived in Brooklyn. We were kids together. He was my best friend.'

My wife was an inveterate tease. 'Isn't that something. I never knew you hung around with juvenile delinquents when you were a kid.'

'He wasn't a juvenile delinquent. Matter of fact –'

'If you aren't the serious one.' She smiled at me in kindly dismissal and went back to Winchell who clearly offered fresher and more exciting tidings than mine. 'Anyhow,' she said, 'I wouldn't let it bother me too much, dear. That was a long time ago.'

It was a long time ago. You could play ball in the middle of the street; few automobiles were to be seen in the far reaches of Brooklyn in 1923. And Bath Beach, where I lived, was one of the farthest reaches. It fronted on Gravesend Bay with Coney Island to the east a few minutes away by trolley car, and Dyker Heights and its golf course to the west a few minutes away by foot. Each was an entity separated from Bath Beach by a wasteland of weed-grown lots which building contractors had not yet discovered.

So, as I said, you could play ball in the streets without fear of traffic. Or you could watch the gas-lighter turning up the street lamps at dusk. Or you could wait around the fire-house on Eighteenth Avenue until, if you were lucky enough, an alarm would send the three big horses there slewing the pump-engine out into the street in a spray of sparks from iron-shod wheels. Or, miracle of miracles, you could stand gaping up at the sky to follow the flight of a biplane proudly racketing along overhead.

Those were the things that I did that summer, along with Iggy Kovac who was my best friend, and who lived in the house next door. It was a two-storey frame house painted in some sedate colour, just as mine was. Most of the houses in Bath Beach were like that, each with a small garden in front and yard in back. The only example of ostentatious architecture on our block was the house on the corner owned by Mr Rose, a newcomer to the neighbourhood. It was huge and stuccoed, almost a mansion, surrounded by an enormous lawn, and with a stuccoed two-car garage at the end of its driveway.

That driveway held a fascination for Iggy and me. On it, now and then, would be parked Mr Rose's automobile, a grey Packard, and it was the car that drew us like a magnet. It was not only beautiful to look at from the distance, but close up it loomed over us like a locomotive, giving off an aura of thunderous power even as it stood there quietly. And it had *two* running-boards, one mounted over the other to make the climb into the tonneau easier. No one else around had anything like that on his car. In fact, no one we knew had a car anywhere near as wonderful as that Packard.

So we would sneak down the driveway when it was parked there, hoping for a chance to mount those running-boards without being caught. We never managed to do it. It seemed that an endless vigil was being kept over that car, either by Mr Rose himself or by someone who lived in the rooms over the garage. As soon as we were no more than a few yards down the driveway a window would open in the house or the garage, and a hoarse voice would bellow threats at us. Then we would turn tail and race down the driveway and out of sight.

We had not always done that. The first time we had seen the car we had sauntered up to it quite casually, all in the spirit of good neighbours, and had not even understood the nature of the threats. We only stood there and looked up in astonishment at Mr Rose, until he suddenly left the window and reappeared before us to grab Iggy's arm.

Iggy tried to pull away and couldn't. 'Leggo of me!' he said in a high-pitched, frightened voice. 'We weren't doing anything to your ole car! Leggo of me, or I'll tell my father on you. Then you'll see what'll happen!'

This did not seem to impress Mr Rose. He shook Iggy back and forth – not hard to do because Iggy was small and skinny even for his age – while I stood there, rooted to the spot in horror.

There were some cranky people in the neighbourhood who would chase us away when we made any noise in front of their houses, but nobody had ever handled either of us or spoken to us the way Mr Rose was doing. I remember having some vague idea that it was because he was new around here, he didn't know yet how people around here were supposed to act, and when I look back now I think I may have been surprisingly close to the truth. But whatever the exact reasons for the storm he raised, it was enough of a storm to have Iggy blubbering out loud, and to make us approach the Packard warily after that. It was too much of a magnet to resist, but once we were on Mr Rose's territory we were like a pair of rabbits crossing open ground during the hunting season. And with just about as much luck.

I don't want to give the impression by all this that we were bad kids. For myself, I was acutely aware of the letter of the law, and had early discovered that the best course for anyone who was good-natured, pacific, and slow afoot – all of which I was in extra measure – was to try and stay within bounds. And Iggy's vices were plain high spirits and recklessness. He was like quicksilver and was always on the go and full of mischief.

And smart. Those were the days when at the end of each school week your marks were appraised and you would be reseated according to your class standing – best students in the first row, next best in the second row, and so on. And I think the thing that best explains Iggy was the way his position in class would fluctuate between the first and sixth rows. Most of us never moved more than one row either way at the end of the week; Iggy would suddenly be shoved from the first row to the ignominy of the sixth, and then the Friday after would just as suddenly ascend the heights back to the first row. That was the sure sign that Mr Kovac had got wind of the bad tidings and had taken measures.

Not physical measures, either. I once asked Iggy about that, and he said, 'Nah, he don't wallop me, but he kind of says don't be so dumb, and, well – you know –'

I did know, because I suspect that I shared a good deal of Iggy's feelings for Mr Kovac, a fervent hero worship. For one thing, most of the fathers in the neighbourhood 'worked in the city' – to use the Bath Beach phrase – meaning that six days a week they ascended the Eighteenth Avenue station of the B.-M.T. and were borne off to desks in Manhattan. Mr Kovac, on the other hand, was a conductor on the Bath Avenue trolley-car line, a powerful and imposing figure in his official cap and blue uniform with the brass buttons on it. The cars on the Bath Avenue line were without side walls, closely lined with benches from front and back, and were manned by conductors who had to swing along narrow platforms on the outside to collect fares. It was something to see Mr Kovac in action. The only thing comparable was the man who swung himself around a Coney Island merry-go-round to take your tickets.

And for another thing, most of the fathers – at least when they had reached the age mine had – were not much on athletics, while Mr Kovac was a terrific baseball player. Every fair Sunday afternoon down at the little park by the bay there was a pick-up ball game where the young fellows of the neighbourhood played a regulation nine innings on a marked-off diamond, and Mr Kovac was always the star. As far as Iggy and I were concerned, he could pitch like Vance and hit like Zack Wheat, and no more than that could be desired. It was something to watch Iggy when his father was at bat. He'd sit chewing his nails right through every windup of the pitcher, and if Mr Kovac came through with a hit, Iggy would be up and screaming so loud you'd think your head was coming off.

Then after the game was over we'd hustle a case of pop over to the team, and they would sit around on the park benches and talk things over. Iggy was his father's shadow then; he'd be hanging around that close to him, taking it all in and eating it up. I wasn't so very far away myself, but since I couldn't claim possession as Iggy could, I amiably kept at a proper distance. And when I went home those afternoons it seemed to me that my father looked terribly stodgy, sitting there on the porch the way he did, with loose pages of the Sunday paper around him.

When I first learned that I was going to have to leave all this, that my family were going to move from Brooklyn to Manhattan, I was completely dazed. Manhattan was a place where on occasional Saturday afternoons you went, all dressed up in your best suit, to shop with your mother at Wanamakers or May's, or, with luck, went to the Hippodrome with your father, or maybe to the Museum of Natural History. It had never struck me as a place where people *lived*.

But as the days went by my feelings changed, became

a sort of apprehensive excitement. After all, I was doing something pretty heroic, pushing off into the Unknown this way, and the glamour of it was brought home to me by the way the kids on the block talked to me about it.

However, none of that meant anything the day before we moved. The house looked strange with everything in it packed and crated and bundled together; my mother and father were in a harried state of mind; and the knowledge of impending change – it was the first time in my life I had ever moved from one house to another – now had me scared stiff.

That was the mood I was in when after an early supper I pushed through the opening in the hedge between our back yard and the Kovacs', and sat down on the steps before their kitchen door. Iggy came out and sat down beside me. He could see how I felt, and it must have made him uncomfortable.

'Jeez, don't be such a baby,' he said. 'It'll be great, living in the city. Look at all the things you'll have to see there.'

I told him I didn't want to see anything there.

'All right, then don't,' he said. 'You want to read something good? I got a new Tarzan, and I got *The Boy Allies at Jutland*. You can have your pick, and I'll take the other one.'

This was a more than generous offer, but I said I didn't feel like reading, either.

'Well, we can't just sit here being mopey,' Iggy said reasonably. 'Let's do something. What do you want to do?'

This was the opening of the ritual where by rejecting various possibilities – it was too late to go swimming, too hot to play ball, too early to go into the house – we would arrive at a choice. We dutifully went through this process of elimination, and it was Iggy as usual who came up with the choice.

'I know,' he said. 'Let's go over to Dyker Heights and fish for golf balls. It's pretty near the best time now, anyhow.'

He was right about that, because the best time to fish for balls that had been driven into the lone water hazard of the course and never recovered by their owners was at sunset, when, chances were, the place would be deserted but there would still be enough light to see by. The way we did this kind of fishing was to pull off our sneakers and stockings, buckle our knickerbockers over our knees, then slowly and speculatively wade through the ooze of the pond, trying to feel out sunken golf balls with our bare feet. It was pleasant work, and occasionally profitable, because the next day any ball you found could be sold to a passing golfer for five cents. I don't remember how we came to fix on the price of five cents as a fair one, but there it was. The golfers seemed to be satisfied with it, and we certainly were.

In all our fishing that summer I don't believe we found more than a total of half a dozen balls, but thirty cents was largesse in those days. My share went fast enough for anything that struck my fancy: Iggy, however, had a great dream. What he wanted more than anything else in the world was a golf club, and every cent he could scrape together was deposited in a tin can with a hole punched in its top and its seam bound with bicycle tape.

He would never open the can, but would shake it now and then to estimate its contents. It was his theory that when the can was full to the top it would hold just about enough to pay for the putter he had picked out in the window of Leo's Sporting Goods Store on 86th Street. Two or three times a week he would have me walk with him down to Leo's, so that we could see the putter, and in between he would talk about it at length, and demonstrate the proper grip for holding it, and the way you have to line up a long putt on a rolling green. Iggy Kovac was the first person I knew – I have known many since – who was really golf crazy. But I think that his case was the most unique, considering that at the time he had never in his life even had his hands on a real club.

So that evening, knowing how he felt about it, I said all right, if he wanted to go fish for golf balls I would go with him. It wasn't much of a walk down Bath Avenue; the only hard part was when we entered the course at its far side where we had to climb over mountains of what was politely called 'fill'. It made hot and smoky going, then there was a swampy patch, and finally the course itself and the water hazard.

I've never been back there since that day, but not long ago I happened to read an article about the Dyker Heights golf course in some magazine or other. According to the article, it was now the busiest public golf course in the world. Its eighteen well-kept greens were packed with players from dawn to dusk, and on weekends you had to get in line at the clubhouse at three or four o'clock in the morning if you wanted a chance to play a round.

Well, each to his own taste, but it wasn't like that when Iggy and I used to fish for golf balls there. For one thing, I don't think it had eighteen holes; I seem to remember it as a nine-hole layout. For another thing, it was usually pretty empty, either because not many people in Brooklyn played golf in those days, or because it was not a very enticing spot at best.

The fact is, it smelled bad. They were reclaiming the swampy land all around it by filling it with refuse, and the smouldering fires in the refuse laid a black pall over the place. No matter when you went there, there was that dirty haze in the air around you, and in a few minutes you'd find your eyes smarting and your nose full of a curious acrid smell.

Not that we minded it, Iggy and I. We accepted it casually as part of the scenery, as much a part as the occasional Mack truck loaded with trash that would rumble along the dirt road to the swamp, its chain-drive chattering and whining as it went. The only thing we did mind sometimes was the heat of the refuse underfoot when we climbed over it. We never dared enter the course from the clubhouse side; the attendant there had once caught us in the pond trying to plunder his preserve, and we knew he had us marked. The back entrance may have been hotter, but it was the more practical way in.

When we reached the pond there was no one else in sight. It was a hot, still evening with a flaming-red sun now dipping toward the horizon, and once we had our sneakers and stockings off – long black cotton stockings they were – we wasted no time wading into the water.

It felt good, too, as did the slick texture of the mud oozing up between my toes when I pressed down. I suspect that I had the spirit of a true fisherman in me then. The pleasure lay in the activity, not in the catch.

Still, the catch made a worthy objective, and the idea was to walk along with slow, probing steps, and to stop whenever you felt anything small and solid underfoot. I had just stopped short with the excited feeling that I had pinned down a golf ball in the muck when I heard the sound of a motor moving along the dirt track nearby. My first thought was that it was one of the dump trucks carrying another load to add to the mountain of filth, but then I knew that it didn't sound like a Mack truck.

I looked around to see what kind of car it was, still keeping my foot planted on my prize, but the row of bunkers between the pond and the road blocked my view. Then the sound of the motor suddenly stopped, and that was all I needed to send me splashing out of the water in a panic. All Iggy needed, too, for that matter. In one second we had grabbed up our shoes and stockings and headed around the corner of the nearest bunker where we would be out of sight. In about five more seconds we had our stockings on without even bothering to dry our legs, ready to take flight if anyone approached.

The reason we moved so fast was simply that we weren't too clear about our legal right to fish for golf balls. Iggy and I had talked it over a couple of times, and while he vehemently maintained that we had every right to – there were the balls, with nobody but the dopey caretaker doing anything about it – he admitted that the smart thing was not to put the theory to the test, but to work at our trade unobserved. And I am sure that when the car stopped nearby he had the same idea I did: somebody had reported us, and now the long hand of authority was reaching out for us.

So we waited, crouching in breathless silence against the grassy wall of the bunker, until Iggy could not contain himself any longer. He crawled on hands and knees to the corner of the bunker and peered around it toward the road. 'Holy smoke, look at that!' he whispered in an awed voice, and waggled his hand at me to come over.

I looked over his shoulder, and with shocked disbelief I saw a grey Packard, a car with double running-boards, one mounted over the other, the only car of its kind I had ever seen. There was no mistaking it, and there was no mistaking Mr Rose who stood with two men near it, talking to the smaller one of them, and making angry chopping motions of his hand as he talked.

Looking back now, I think that what made the scene such a strange one was its setting. There was the deserted golf course all around us, and the piles of smouldering fill in the distance, everything seeming so raw and uncitylike and made crimson by the setting sun; and there in the middle of it was this sleek car and the three men with straw hats and jackets and neckties, all looking completely out of place.

Even more fascinating was the smell of danger around them, because while I couldn't hear what was being said I could see that Mr Rose was in the same mood he had been in when he caught Iggy and me in his driveway. The big man next to him said almost nothing, but the little man Mr Rose was talking to shook his head, tried to answer, and kept backing away slowly, so that Mr Rose had to follow him. Then suddenly the little man wheeled around and ran right toward the bunker where Iggy and I were hidden.

We ducked back, but he ran past the far side of it, and he was almost past the pond when the big man caught up with him and grabbed him, Mr Rose running up after them with his hat in his hand. That is when we could have got away without being seen, but we didn't. We crouched there spellbound, watching something we would never have dreamed of seeing – grown-ups having it out right in front of us the way it happened in the movies.

I was, as I have said, twelve years old that summer. I can now mark it as the time I learned that there was a difference between seeing things in the movies and seeing them in real life. Because never in watching the most bruising movie, with Tom Mix or Hoot Gibson or any of my heroes, did I feel what I felt there watching what happened to that little man. And I think that Iggy must have felt it even more acutely than I did, because he was so small and skinny himself, and while he was tough in a fight he was always being outweighed and overpowered. He must have felt that he was right there inside that little man, his arms pinned tight behind his back by the bully who had grabbed him, while Mr Rose hit him back and forth with an open hand across the face, snarling at him all the while.

'You dirty dog,' Mr Rose said. 'Do you know who I am? Do you think I'm one of those lousy small-time bootleggers you double-cross for the fun of it? *This* is who I am!' And with the little man screaming and kicking out at him he started punching as hard as he could at the belly and face until the screaming and kicking suddenly stopped. Then he jerked his head toward the pond, and his pal heaved the little man right into it headfirst, the straw hat flying off and bobbing up and down in the water a few feet away.

They stood watching until the man in the water managed to get on his hands and knees, blowing out dirty water, shaking his head in a daze, and then without another word they walked off toward the car, I heard its doors slam, and the roar of the motor as it moved off, and then the sound faded away.

All I wanted to do then was get away from there. What I had just seen was too much to comprehend or even believe in; it was like waking up from a nightmare to find it real. Home was where I wanted to be.

I stood up cautiously, but before I could scramble off to home and safety, Iggy clutched the back of my shirt so hard that he almost pulled me down on top of him.

'What're you doing?' he whispered hotly. 'Where do you think you're going?'

I pulled myself free. 'Are you crazy?' I whispered back. 'You expect to hang around here all night? I'm going home, that's where I'm going.'

Iggy's face was ashy white, his nostrils flaring. 'But that guy's hurt. You just gonna let him stay there?'

'Sure I'm gonna let him stay there. What's it my business?'

'You saw what happened. You think it's right to beat up a guy like that?'

What he said and the way he said it in a tight, choked voice made me wonder if he really had gone crazy just then. I said weakly, 'It's none of my business, that's all. Anyhow, I have to go home. My folks'll be sore if I don't get home on time.'

Iggy pointed an accusing finger at me. 'All right, if that's the way you feel!' he said, and then before I could stop him he turned and dashed out of concealment toward the pond. Whether it was the sense of being left alone in a hostile world, or whether it was some wild streak of loyalty that acted on me, I don't know. But I hesitated only an instant and then ran after him.

He stood at the edge of the pond looking at the man in it who was still on his hands and knees and shaking his head vaguely from side to side. 'Hey, mister,' Iggy said, and there was none of the assurance in his voice that there had been before, 'are you hurt?'

The man looked slowly around at us, and his face was fearful to behold. It was bruised and swollen and glassy-eyed, and his dripping hair hung in long strings down his forehead. It was enough to make Iggy and me back up a step, the way he looked.

With a great effort he pushed himself to his feet and stood there swaying. Then he lurched forward, staring at us blindly, and we hastily backed up a few more steps. He stopped short and suddenly reached down and scooped up a handful of mud from under the water.

'Get out of here!' he cried out like a woman screaming. 'Get out of here, you little sneaks!' – and without warning flung mud at us.

It didn't hit me, but it didn't have to. I let out one yell of panic and ran wildly, my heart thudding, my legs pumping as fast as they could. Iggy was almost at my shoulder – I could hear him gasping as we climbed the smouldering hill of refuse that barred the way to the avenue, slid down the other side in a cloud of dirt and ashes, and raced toward the avenue without looking back. It was only when we reached the first streetlight that we stopped and stood there trembling, our mouths wide open, trying to suck in air, our clothes fouled from top to bottom.

But the shock I had undergone was nothing compared to what I felt when Iggy finally got his wind back enough to speak up.

'Did you see that guy?' he said, still struggling for breath, 'Did you see what they did to him? Come on, I'm gonna tell the cops.'

I couldn't believe my ears. 'The cops? What do you want to get mixed up with the cops for? What do you care what they did to him, for Pete's sake?'

'Because they beat him up, didn't they? And the cops can stick them in jail for fifty years if somebody tells them, and I'm a witness. I saw what happened and so did you. So you're a witness too.'

I didn't like it. I certainly had no sympathy for the evil-looking apparition from which I had just fled, and, more than that, I balked at the idea of having anything to do with the police. Not that I had ever had any trouble with them. It was just that, like most other kids I knew, I was nervous in the presence of a police uniform. It left me even more mystified by Iggy than ever. The idea of any kid voluntarily walking up to report something to a policeman was beyond comprehension.

I said bitterly, 'All right, so I'm a witness. But why can't the guy that got beat up go and tell the cops about it? Why do we have to go and do it?'

'Because he wouldn't tell anybody about it. Didn't you see the way he was scared of Mr Rose? You think it's all right for Mr Rose to go around like that, beating up anybody he wants to, and nobody does anything about it?'

Then I understood. Beneath all this weird talk, this sudden access of nobility, was solid logic, something I could get hold of. It was not the man in the water Iggy was concerned with, it was himself. Mr Rose had pushed *him* around, and now he had a perfect way of getting even.

I didn't reveal this thought to Iggy, though, because when your best friend has been shoved around and humiliated in front of you, you don't want to remind him of it. But at least it put everything into proper perspective. Somebody hurts you, so you hurt him back, and that's all there is to it.

It also made it much easier to go along with Iggy in his plan. I wasn't really being called on to ally myself with some stupid grown-up who had got into trouble with Mr Rose; I was being a good pal to Iggy.

All of a sudden, the prospect of walking into the police station and telling my story to somebody seemed highly intriguing. And, the reassuring thought went, far in the back of my head, none of this would mean trouble for me later on, because tomorrow I was moving to Manhattan anyhow, wasn't I?

So I was right there, a step behind Iggy, when we walked up between the two green globes which still seemed vaguely menacing to me, and into the police station. There was a tall desk there, like a judge's bench, at which a grey-haired man sat writing, and at its foot was another desk at which sat a very fat uniformed man reading a magazine. He put the magazine down when we approached and looked at us with raised eyebrows.

'Yeah?' he said. 'What's the trouble?'

I had been mentally rehearsing a description of what I had seen back there on the golf course, but I never had a chance to speak my piece. Iggy started off with a rush, and there was no way of getting a word in. The fat man listened with a puzzled expression, every now and then pinching his lower lip between his thumb and forefinger. Then he looked up at the one behind the tall desk and said, 'Hey, sergeant, here's a couple of kids say they saw an assault over at Dyker Heights. You want to listen to this?'

The sergeant didn't even look at us, but kept on writing. 'Why?' he said. 'What's wrong with your ears?'

The fat policeman leaned back in his chair and smiled. 'I don't know,' he said, 'only it seems to me some guy named Rose is mixed up in this.'

The sergeant suddenly stopped writing. 'What's that?' he said.

'Some guy named Rose,' the fat policeman said, and he appeared to be enjoying himself a good deal. 'You know anybody with that name who drives a big grey Packard?'

The sergeant motioned with his head for us to come right up to the platform his desk was on. 'All right, kid,' he said to Iggy, 'what's bothering you?'

So Iggy went through it again, and when he was finished the sergeant just sat there looking at him, tapping his pen on the desk. He looked at him so long and kept tapping that pen so steadily – tap, tap, tap – that my skin started to crawl. It didn't surprise me when he finally said to Iggy in a hard voice, 'You're a pretty wise kid.'

'What do you mean?' Iggy said. 'I *saw* it!' He pointed at me. 'He saw it, too. He'll tell you!'

I braced myself for the worst and then noted with relief that the sergeant was paying no attention to me. He shook his head at Iggy and said, 'I do the telling around here, kid. And I'm telling you you've got an awful big mouth for someone your size. Don't you have more sense than to go around trying to get people into trouble?'

This, I thought, was the time to get away from there, because if ever I needed proof that you don't mix into grown-up business I had it now. But Iggy didn't budge. He was always pretty good at arguing himself out of spots where he was wrong; now that he knew he was right he was getting hot with outraged virtue.

'Don't you believe me?' he demanded. 'For Pete's sake, I was right there when it happened! I was this close!'

The sergeant looked like a thundercloud. 'All right, you were that close,' he said. 'Now beat it, kid, and keep that big mouth shut. I got no time to fool around any more. Go on, get out of here.'

Iggy was so enraged that not even the big gold badge a foot from his nose could intimidate him now. 'I don't care if you don't believe me!' he said. 'There's plenty other people'll believe me. Wait'll I tell my father. You'll see!'

I could hear my ears ringing in the silence that followed. The sergeant sat staring at Iggy, and Iggy, a little scared by his own outburst, stared back. He must have had the same idea I did then. Yelling at a cop was probably as bad as hitting one, and we'd both end up in jail for the rest of our lives. Not for a second did I feel any of the righteous indignation Iggy did. As far as I was concerned, he had led me into this trap, and I was going to pay for this lunacy. I guess I hated him then even more than the sergeant did.

It didn't help any when the sergeant finally turned to the fat policeman with the air of a man who had made up his mind.

'Take the car and drive over to Rose's place,' he said. 'You can explain all this to him, and ask him to come along back with you. Oh yes, and get this kid's name and address, and bring his father along, too. Then we'll see.'

So I had my first and only experience of sitting on a bench in a police station watching the pendulum of the big clock on the wall swinging back and forth, and re-counting all my past sins to myself. It couldn't have been more than a half hour before the fat policeman walked in with Mr Rose and Iggy's father, but it seemed like a year. And a long, miserable year at that.

The surprising thing was the way Mr Rose looked. I had half expected them to bring him in fighting and struggling, because while the sergeant may not have believed Iggy's story Mr Rose would know it was so.

But far from struggling, Mr Rose looked as if he had dropped in for a friendly visit. He was dressed in a fine summer suit and sporty-looking black and white shoes and he was smoking a cigar. He was perfectly calm and pleasant, and, in some strange way, he almost gave the impression that he was in charge there.

It was different with Iggy's father. Mr Kovac must have been reading the paper out on the porch in his undershirt, because his regular shirt had been stuffed into his pants carelessly and part of it hung out. And from his manner you'd think that he was the one who had done something wrong. He kept swallowing hard, and twisting his neck in his collar, and now and then glancing nervously at Mr Rose. He didn't look at all impressive as he did at other times.

The sergeant pointed at Iggy. 'All right, kid,' he said 'now tell everybody here what you told me. Stand up so we can all hear it.'

Since Iggy had already told it twice he really had it down pat now, and he told it without a break from start to finish, no one interrupting him. And all the while Mr Rose stood there listening politely, and Mr Kovac kept twisting his neck in his collar.

When Iggy was finished the sergeant said, 'I'll put it to you straight out, Mr Rose. Were you near that golf course today?'

Mr Rose smiled. 'I was not,' he said.

'Of course not,' said the sergeant. 'But you can see what we're up against here.'

'Sure I can,' said Mr Rose. He went over to Iggy and put a hand on his shoulder. 'And you know what?' he said. 'I don't even blame the kid for trying this trick. He and I had a little trouble some time back about the way he was always climbing over my car, and I guess he's just trying to get square with me. I'd say he's got a lot of spirit in him. Don't you, sonny?' he asked, squeezing Iggy's shoulder in a friendly way.

I was stunned by the accuracy of this shot, but Iggy reacted like a firecracker going off. He pulled away from Mr Rose's hand and ran over to his father. 'I'm not lying!' he said desperately and grabbed Mr Kovac's shirt, tugging at it. 'Honest to God, pop, we both saw it. Honest to God, pop!'

Mr Kovac looked down at him and then looked around at all of us. When his eyes were on Mr Rose it seemed as if his collar were tighter than ever. Meanwhile, Iggy was pulling at his shirt, yelling that we saw it, we saw it, and he wasn't lying, until Mr Kovac shook him once, very hard, and that shut him up.

'Iggy,' said Mr Kovac, 'I don't want you to go around telling stories about people. Do you hear me?'

Iggy heard him, all right. He stepped back as if he had been walloped across the face, and then stood there looking at Mr Kovac in a funny way. He didn't say anything, didn't even move when Mr Rose came up and put a hand on his shoulder again.

'You heard your father, didn't you, kid?' Mr Rose said.

Iggy still didn't say anything.

'Sure you did,' Mr Rose said. 'And you and I understand each other a lot better now, kiddo, so there's no hard feelings. Matter of fact, any time you want to come over to the house you come on over, and I'll bet there's plenty of odd jobs you can do there. I pay good, too, so don't you worry about that.' He reached into his pocket and took out a bill. 'Here,' he said, stuffing it into Iggy's hand, 'this'll give you an idea. Now go on out and have yourself some fun.'

Iggy looked at the money like a sleepwalker. I was baffled by that. As far as I could see, this was the business, and here was Iggy in a daze, instead of openly rejoicing. It was only when the sergeant spoke to us that he seemed to wake up.

'All right, you kids,' the sergeant said, 'beat it home now. The rest of us got some things to talk over.'

I didn't need a second invitation. I got out of there in a hurry and went down the street fast, with Iggy tagging along behind me not saying a word. It was three blocks down and one block over, and I didn't slow down until I was in front of my house again. I had never appreciated those familiar outlines and the lights in the windows any more than I did at that moment. But I didn't go right in. It suddenly struck me that this was the last time I'd be seeing Iggy, so I waited there awkwardly. I was never very good at saying good-byes.

'That was all right,' I said finally. 'I mean Mr Rose giving you that dollar. That's as good as twenty golf balls.'

'Yeah?' said Iggy, and he was looking at me in the same funny way he had looked at his father. 'I'll bet it's as good as a whole new golf club. Come on down to Leo's with me, and I'll show you.'

I wanted to, but I wanted to get inside the house even more. 'Ahh, my folks'll be sore if I stay out too late tonight,' I said. 'Anyway, you can't buy a club for a dollar. You'll need way more than that.'

'You think so?' Iggy said, and then held out his hand and slowly opened it so that I could see what he was holding. It was not a one-dollar bill. It was, to my awe, a five-dollar bill.

That, as my wife said, was a long time ago. Thirty-five years before a photograph was taken of little Ignace Kovac, a man wise in the way of the rackets, slumped in a death agony over the wheel of his big car, a bullet hole in the middle of his forehead, a bag of golf clubs leaning against the seat next to him. Thirty-five years before I understood the meaning of the last things said and done when we faced each other on a street in Brooklyn, and then went off, each in his own direction.

I gaped at the money in Iggy's hand. It was the hoard of Croesus, and its very magnitude alarmed me.

'Hey,' I said. 'That's five bucks. That's a lot of money! You better give it to your old man, or he'll really jump on you.'

Then I saw to my surprise that the hand holding the money was shaking. Iggy was suddenly shuddering all over as if he had just plunged into icy water.

'My old man?' he yelled wildly at me, and his lips drew back showing his teeth clenched together hard, as if that could stop the shuddering. 'You know what I'll do if my old man tries anything? I'll tell Mr Rose on him, that's what! Then you'll see!'

And wheeled and ran blindly away from me down the street to his destiny.

The Liar

William Faulkner

Four men sat comfortably on the porch of Gibson's store, facing the railroad tracks and two nondescript yellow buildings. The two buildings belonged to the railroad company, hence they were tidy in an impersonal way, and were painted the same prodigious yellow. The store, not belonging to the railroad company, was not painted. It squatted stolidly against a rising hill, so that the proprietor could sit at ease, spitting into the valley, and watch the smoke-heralded passing of casual trains. The store and the proprietor resembled each other, slovenly and comfortable; and it was seldom that the owner's was the only chair tilted against the wall, and his the only shavings littering the floor.

Today he had four guests. Two of these had ridden in from the hills for trivial necessities, the other two had descended from the morning's local freight; and they sat in easy amity, watching the smoke from the locomotive dwindle away down the valley.

'Who's that feller, coming up from the deepo?' spoke one at last. The others followed his gaze and the stranger mounted the path from the station under their steady provincial stare. He was roughly dressed – a battered felt hat, a coarse blue cloth jacket and corduroy trousers – a costume identical with that of at least one of the watchers.

'Never seen him before. He don't live hereabouts, that I know of,' murmured the proprietor. 'Any of you boys know him?'

They shook their heads. 'Might be one of them hill fellers. They stays back yonder all the year round, some of 'em ain't never been out.' The speaker, a smallish man with a large round bald head and a long saturnine face in which his two bleached eyes were innocent and keen – like a depraved priest – continued: 'Feller over to Mitchell says one of 'em brung his whole family into town one day last month to let 'em see a train. Train blowed, and his wife and six-seven children started milling round kind of nervous; but when she come in sight around the bend the whole bunch broke for the woods.

'Old man Mitchell himself had drove down fer his paper, and them hill folks run right spang over his outfit: tore his buggy all to pieces and scart his hoss so bad it took 'em till next day noon to catch him. Yes, sir, heard 'em whooping and hollering all night, trying to head that hoss into something with a fence around it. They say he run right through old Mis' Harmon's house –' The narrator broke down over his own invention. His audience laughed too, enjoying the humour, but tolerantly, as one laughs at a child. His fabling was well known. And though like all peoples who live close to the soil, they were by nature veracious, they condoned his unlimited imagination for the sake of the humour he achieved and which they understood.

The laughter ceased, for the newcomer was near. He mounted the shaky steps and stood among them, a dark-favoured man. 'Morning, gentlemen,' he greeted them without enthusiasm.

The proprietor, as host, returned his greeting. The others muttered something, anything, as was the custom. The stranger entered the store and the owner rose reluctantly and luxuriously to follow him.

'Say,' spoke the raconteur, 'ever notice how spry Will is for trade? See him jump up when a customer comes in, and nigh tromps his heels off herding him inside? Minds me of the time –'

'Shet up, Ek,' another told him equably. 'You already told one lie this morning. Give a man time to smoke a pipe betwixt 'em, leastways. Mebbe that stranger'd like to hear ye. And Will'd hate to miss it, too.' The others guffawed, and spat.

Gibson and his customer returned; the proprietor sank with a sigh into his chair and the other, bearing a piece of cheese and a paper sack of crackers, lowered himself onto the top step, his back against a post, partly facing them. He began his meal while they stared at him, gravely and without offence, as children, and all whose desires and satisfactions are simple, can.

'Say, Will,' said one after a while, 'you come near missing one of Ek's yarns. Us fellers stopped him, though. Now, Ek, you kin go ahead.'

'Lissen,' said the one called Ek, readily, 'all you boys think that ever' time I open my mouth it's to do a little blanket stretching, but lemme tell you something cur'ous that reely happened. 'Twas like this –'

He was interrupted. 'H'y, Will, git out yer hoss medicine: Ek's took sick.'

'Musta had a stroke. We kept telling him ter stay outa them sunny fields.'

'Yes, sir; shows what work'll do fer you.'

'No, boys, it's that licker them Simpson boys makes: Makes a man tell the truth all the time. Sho' better keep it outen the courts, or ever'body'll be in jail.'

Ek had vainly striven to surmount the merriment. 'You fellers don't know nothing,' he roared. 'Feller comes trying to tell you the truth –' They shouted him down again, and Will Gibson summed the matter up.

'Why, Ek, we ain't doubting your ability to tell the truth when it's necessary, like in court or meeting house; but they ain't no truth ever happened as entertaining as your natural talk, hey boys? He's better'n a piece in the theayter, ain't he, fellers?'

The others assented loudly, but Ek refused to be mollified. He sat in offended dignity. The others chuckled at intervals, but at last the merriment was gone and there was no sound save the stranger's methodical crunching. He, seemingly, had taken no part in the laughter. Far up the valley a train whistled; echo took the sound and toyed with it, then let it fade back into silence.

But silence was unbearable to Ek. At last it overcame his outraged dignity. 'Say,' he went easily into narrative, 'lemme tell you something cur'ous that reely happened to me yest'day. I was over to Mitchell yest'day waiting for the early local, when I meets up with Ken Rogers, the sheriff. We passed the time of day and he says to me, what am I doing today, and I tells him I aim to ride No. 12 over home. Then he says he's looking for somebody like me, asking me wasn't I raised in the hills. I tells him I was, and how when I turned twenty-one, paw decided I had ought to wear shoes. I hadn't never worn no shoes, and was young and skittish as a colt in them days.

'Well, sir, you may believe it or not, but when they come to my pallet that morning with them new shoes, I up and lit out of there in my shirt tail and took to the woods. Paw sent word around to the neighbours and they organized a hunt same as a bear hunt, with axes and ropes and dogs. No guns, though; paw held that to shoot me would be a waste of manpower, as I could stand up to a day's work with any of 'em.

'Well, sir, it took 'em two days to git me, and they only got me then when them big man-eating hounds of Lem Haley's put me up a tree in Big Sandy bottom, twenty miles from home. And mebbe you won't believe it, but it took paw and three strong men to put them shoes on me.' He led the laughter himself, which the stranger joined. 'Yes, sir; them was the days. But lemme see, I kind of got off the track. Where was I? Oh, yes. Well, the sheriff he says to me can't I go back into the hills a ways with him. And I says, well, I dunno; I got some business in Sidon to tend to today –'

'Same business you're tending to now, I reckon?' interrupted one of his audience. 'Got to git back where folks believe him when he says he's telling the truth.'

'Now, look-a-here,' began the affronted narrator, when the proprietor interfered. 'Hush up, you Lafe; let him finish his tale. G'on, Ek, won't nobody bother you again.'

Ek looked at him in gratitude and resumed. 'Well, listen. The sheriff, he says to me, he needs a man that knows them hill folks to go in with him. Been some trouble of some kind and he wants to clear it up. But them hill people is so leary that they's liable to shoot first, before a man kin state his point. So he wants I should go along with him and kind of mollify 'em, you might say, promising to get me back in time to catch the evening train. Well, they ain't nothing I couldn't put off a day or so, so I goes with him. He's got his car all ready and a deppity waiting, so we piles in and lit out.

'It was as putty a day as I ever see and we was having a good time, laughing and talking back and forth –'

Lafe interrupted again: 'Must of been, with a set of fellers't never heard your lies before.'

'Be quiet, Lafe,' Gibson commanded peremptorily.

'– and first thing I knew, we come to a place where the road played out altogether. "Have to walk from here on," sheriff says, so we runs the car off the road a ways, and struck out afoot. Well, sir, I was born and raised in them hills, but I never seen that stretch where we was before – all ridges, and gullies where you could sling a hoss off and lose him. Finally the sheriff says to me: "Ek," he says, "place we're heading for is jest across that ridge. You go on over to the house, and tell Mrs Starnes who you are; and Tim and me'll go around yonder way. Probably catch Joe in his lower field. We'll meet you at the house. Might ask Mis' Starnes if she kin git us a little snack ready." '

'All right, sheriff,' I says, 'but I don't know nobody through here.'

' "That's all right," sheriff says, "jest go up to the house and tell her me and Joe and Tim'll be 'long soon." And him and Tim started on around the ridge, and I took the route he give me. Well, sir, I moseyed on up to the top of the ridge, and sho' 'nough, there was a house and a barn setting in the next valley. It didn't look like much of a farm and I just decided them Starneses was average shif'less hill folks. There was a lot of rocks on the ridge where I was, and just as I was thinking what a good place for snakes it was and starting on down to'rds the house – bzzzrrr! went something right behind me. Gentlemen, I jumped twenty foot and lit grabbing rocks. When I had throwed a couple the rattler was gone into a hole; and then I seen three others laying with their heads smashed, and I knowed I must of stumbled into a regular den of 'em. They hadn't been dead long, and from the sample I'd had I knowed how mad the others must be, so I lit a shuck out of there. But I wasn't far from the feller had killed them three, but just how close I never learnt till later.

'I dropped on down through the brush, coming to the

house from behind. Down the hill from the barn and between me and the house was a spring in a rocky gully. The spring was railed off from cattle. There was gullies and rocks ever'where: I never seen such pore, rocky land – sink holes full of rocks and narrer as wells. I had to jump 'em like a goat.

'I was about half-way down the hill when I seen a feller moving down at the spring. I hadn't seen him before. He jest wasn't there when I looked once, but there he was when I looked again, rising up by the spring. He had a wooden box under his arm. I never knowed where he come from.

'Knowing how skittish them hill folks are, I was jest about to sing out when he put his finger in his mouth and whistled. I thought mebbe he was calling his dog, and I was thinking to myself it was a sorry dog that never suspicioned me when I was this close, when a woman come to the back door of the house. She stood there a minute, shading her eyes and looking all around at the ridges, but she never did look to'rds the spring. Then she stepped out, toting something in her hand, and started fer the spring on the run. Then I could see she had her Sunday hat on, and that the thing in her hand was a carpetbag. Fellers, she jest flew down that hill.

' "Uh, uh," thinks I to myself, "they's something going on here that I don't know about, and that Starnes don't know nothing about, neither." The sheriff seemed mighty certain he wouldn't be to home, and I never seen a man and wife go to all that trouble to go anywheres.

'Well, sir, they met at the spring. The feller had set his little box down careful, and they was clamped together like two sheep in a storm, and was a-kissing. "Uh, uh!" thinks I, "here's something else me and Starnes don't know about, and what'd make him itch if he did." I was higher up than them two, and I taken a look around fer sheriff and Tim, and I seen a lone feller coming down the valley. They couldn't see him a tall, but jest when I seen him, he spied them. He stopped a minute like he was studying, then he come, not hiding exactly, but walking careful.

'Meanwhile, them two at the spring was bent over the feller's little box, and I seen her jump back and kind of squeal. Well, sir, things was getting cur'ouser and cur'ouser ever' minute, and I was a-wishing and a-griping for sheriff and Tim to git there. "If sheriff's wanting something to clear up," I thinks to myself, "I got it here waiting fer him." And about then things begun to pop.

'Them two at the spring looked up all on a sudden. They had either seen or heard the other feller; so he walked in bold as you please. The woman she kind of comes behind the first feller; then she drops her bag and makes a bee-line fer the other one, the feller that jest come up, and tries to grab him round the neck. He flings her off and she fell flat, but jumped up and tried to grab him again.

'Well, sir, she kep' on trying to hold his arm and he kep' on a-flinging her off, all the time walking not fast but steady to'rds number one. Finally she sees she can't stop 'em, so she backed off with her hands kind of against her side, and I can see she is scared most to death. Them two fellers is about a yard apart, when number two hauled off and knocked the other one clean into the spring. He jumped up right away and grabbed up a rail from the fence that kep' cattle out of the spring. The woman hollered and grabbed at number two again, and while he was shaking her loose, number one ups and hits him over the head with his rail, and he dropped like a ox. Them hill folks has got hard heads, but it seemed to me I could hear that feller's skull bust. Leastways, he never moved again. The woman backed off, clamping her head betwixt her hands; and the feller watched him awhile then throwed away his rail.

'Well, sir, you could of knocked me down with a straw. There I was, watching murder, skeered to move, and no sign of sheriff and Tim. I've got along fine without no law officers, but I sho' needed one then.' Ek stopped, with consummate art, and gazed about on his hearers. Their eyes were enraptured on his face, the hot black gaze of the stranger seemed like a blade spitting him against the wall, like a pinned moth. The train whistled again, unheard.

'Go on, go on,' breathed Gibson.

He drew his gaze from the stranger's by an effort of will, and found that the pleasant May morning was suddenly chill. For some reason he did not want to continue.

'Well, sir, I didn't know whether the feller would finish his job right then or not; seemed like he didn't know himself. And all the time the woman was like she was took by a spell. Finally he walked over and picked the unconscious feller up, and carried him about fifteen foot down the gully, then dumped him like a sack of meal into one of them narrow sink holes. And all the time the woman was watching him like she was turned to stone.' The train whistled again and the locomotive came in sight, but not one turned his eyes from the narrator's face.

'Seemed like he had decided what to do know. He run back to'rds where the woman was, and I thinks, my God, he's going to kill her, too. But no, he's jest after his box. He grabs it up and come back to where he had throwed the other feller. Well, sir, if I could have been cur'ous over anything right then, I would have been cur'ous over what he was a-doing now. But as it was, I was past thinking; jest goggle-eyed, like a fish when you jerk him out the water.

'And all the time this feller is fiddling with his box, standing on the edge of that sink hole. All on a sudden he helt it out from him, shaking it over the hole. Finally something all knotted and shiny like a big watch chain fell out of it and dropped, shining and twisting, into the place where the other feller was.

'Then I knowed who'd killed them rattlers.'

'My God,' said someone.

'Yes, sir. They'd planned to fix that there snake where number two'd stumble on it when he come in, only he come too soon for 'em.'

'My God!' repeated the voice, then the one called Lafe screamed:

'Look out!'

A pistol said whow, the sound slammed against the front of the store and roared against the porch. Ek rolled from his chair and thumped on the floor, tried to rise, and fell again. Lafe sprang erect, but the others sat in reft and silent amaze, watching the stranger leaping down the path toward the track and the passing train; saw him recklessly grasp a car ladder and, shaving death by inches, scramble aboard.

Later, when the doctor had ridden ten miles, dressed Ek's shoulder, cursed him for a fool, and gone, the four of them took him to task.

'Well, Ek, I guess you learnt your lesson. You'll know better than tell the truth again.'

'Ain't it the beatingest thing? Here's a man lied his way through life fer forty years and never got a scratch, then sets out to tell the truth fer once in his life, and gets shot.'

'But what was your point,' Will Gibson reiterated, 'in telling your fool yarn right in front of the feller that did it? Didn't you know him again?'

Ek turned his fever exasperated face to them. 'I tell you that it was all a lie, ever last word of it. I wasn't nowhere near Mitchell yest'day.'

They shook their heads at his obstinacy; then Gibson, seeing that they were increasing the patient's fever, drove them out. The last to go, he turned at the door for a parting shot.

'I don't know whether you were lying, or were telling the truth, but either way, you must get a whole lot of satisfaction out of this. If you were lying, you ought to be shot for telling one so prob'le that it reely happened somewhere; and if you were telling the truth, you ought to be shot for having no better sense than to blab it out in front of the man that done the killing. Either way, if you ain't learnt a lesson, I have. And that is, don't talk at all lessen you have to, and when you got to talk, tell the truth.'

'Aw, get out of here,' snarled Ek. And convicted of both truthfulness and stupidity, he turned his face bitterly to the wall, knowing that his veracity as a liar was gone forever.

It Takes a Thief

Arthur Miller

Some people are laughing in our neighbourhood these nights, but most of us are just waiting, like the Sheltons. It is simply unbelievable, it came out so right.

Here is this man, Mr Shelton, a middle-aged man with what they call a nice family and a nice home. Ordinary kind of businessman, tired every night, sit around on Sundays, pinochle and so on. The point is, he's been doing all right the past few year. Automobiles. His used cars are shipped to California, Florida – wherever the war plants were springing up. Did fine. Then the war ended. The new cars started coming through and then the strikes made them scarce. But people wanted them very badly. Very, very badly. He did fine. Very, very fine.

One night not long ago he and his wife decided to take in a night club, and she put on her two diamond rings, the bracelet, and some of her other frozen cash, and they locked up the house – the children are all married and don't live home any more – and they were off for a trip to the city.

Nobody knows what they did in the city, but they stayed out till 3 in the morning. Late enough for Shelton to get a headful. The drive home was slow and careful because the car was one of his brand-new ones and he couldn't see too well in his condition. Nevertheless, when he put the key in the front door lock he was able to notice that the door swung open at a touch, whereas it usually took some juggling of the latch. They went in and turned on the living room lights, and then they saw it.

The drawer of the desk was lying on the floor, and the

rug was littered with cheque stubs and stationery. The Sheltons rushed into the dining room and saw at once that the sterling silver service was gone from the massive serving table. Shelton clutched at his heart as though he were going to suffocate, and Mrs Shelton thrust her fingers into her hair and screamed. At this stage, of course, there was only the sensation that an alien presence had passed through their home. Perhaps they even imagined that the thief was still there. In wild fright they ran to the stairs and up to their bedroom, and Shelton tripped and fell over a bureau drawer that the thief had left on the threshold. Mrs Shelton helped him up and made him lie down on the colonial bed and she massaged his heart while they both looked anxiously towards the closet door, which stood open.

When he had caught his breath, he pushed her aside and went into the closet and turned on the light. She crowded in beside him as soon as she saw the terrible expression on his face. The safe. The little steel safe that had always stood in the corner of the closet covered with dress boxes and old clothes, the safe was looking up at them from the corner with its door open. Shelton simply stood there panting. It was Mrs Shelton who got to her knees and felt inside.

Nothing. Nothing was left. The safe was empty. Mrs Shelton, on her knees in the closet, screamed again. Perhaps they felt once more the presence, the terrifying presence of the thief, for they rushed one behind the other down the stairs, and Shelton picked up the telephone.

The instrument shook in his hand as he bent over close to the dial and spun it around. Mrs Shelton moved up and down beside him, clasping and unclasping her hands and weeping. 'Oh, my God!'

'Police!' Shelton roared into the telephone as soon as he heard the operator's calm voice. 'My house has been robbed. We just got home and –'

His voice caught Mrs Shelton just as she was about to dig her fingers into her hair again. For an instant she stood perfectly still, then she turned suddenly and swung her arm out and clapped her hand over Shelton's mouth. Infuriated, he attempted to knock her hand away. Then his eyes met hers. They stood that way, looking into each other's eyes; and then Shelton's hand began to shake violently and he dropped the telephone with a loud bang onto the marble tabletop and collapsed into a high-backed Italian-type chair. Mrs Shelton replaced the telephone on its cradle as the operator's anxious voice flowed out of it.

They were both too frightened to speak for a few minutes. The same thing was rushing through their heads and there was no need to say what it was. Only a solution was needed, and neither of them could find it. At last Mrs Shelton said, 'You didn't give the operator the name or address. Maybe –'

'We'll see,' he said, and went into the living room and stretched out on the couch.

Mrs Shelton went to the front windows and drew the shades. Then she came back to the couch and proceeded to walk up and down beside it, her breasts rising and falling with the heavy rhythm of her breathing.

Nothing happened for nearly an hour. They even made a pass at undressing, just as though he had not shouted frantically into the telephone that his house had been robbed. But they were hardly out of their clothes when the doorbell rang. In dressing gown and slippers Shelton went down the stairs with his wife behind him. In the presence of strangers he always knew how to look calm, so much so that when he opened the door and let the two policemen in, he appeared almost sleepy.

The question of his having hung up without giving his name was cleared away first: he had been too excited to give that detail to the operator. The officers then went about inspecting the premises. That completed, Shelton and his wife sat in the living room with them and gave a detailed description of seven pieces of jewellery that had been taken from the safe, and the silver service, and the old Persian lamb coat, and the other items, all of which were noted in a black-covered pad that one policeman wrote in. When Shelton had closed the door behind the two officers, he stood thinking for awhile, and his wife waited for his word. Finally he said, 'We'll report the jewellery to the insurance company tomorrow.'

'What about the money?'

'How can I mention the money?'

She knew there was no answer to that one, but it was hard, nevertheless, to give up $91,000 without a complaint.

In bed they lay without moving. Thinking. 'What'll we do,' she asked, 'if they find the crook and he's still got the money?'

A long time later, Shelton said, 'They never catch thieves.'

Eight days passed, in fact, before Shelton's opinion was proved wrong. The telephone rang at dinnertime. He covered the mouthpiece with his palm and turned to his wife. 'They want me to come down and identify the stuff.' There was a quavering note in his voice.

'What about the money?' she whispered.

'They didn't mention the money,' he said, questioning her with his eyes.

'Maybe tell them you're too sick to go now.'

'I'll have to go sometime.'

'Try to find out first if they found the money.'

'I can't *ask* them, can I?' he said angrily, and turned again to the telephone and said he would be right over.

He drove slowly. The new, purring engine, the $1,900 car for which he could easily get $4,000 cash carried him effortlessly towards the police station. He drove slumped in the seat. As though to rehearse, he kept repeating the same sentence in his mind: I am simply a dealer, I am simply a dealer; I kept that much cash on hand to buy cars with. It sounded all right, businesslike. But was it possible they were that dumb? Maybe. They were just plain cops. Plain cops might not realize that $91,000 was too much to have in a safe for that purpose. And still, it was possible they would not stumble on the truth at all, not know that cash in a home safe was probably not entered on any ledger or income-tax form. Cops did not know much about big money, he felt. And yet – $91,000. Oh! $91,000! His insides grew cool at the thought of it. Not $20,000 or 40,000, not even 75,000, but $91,000. His retirement, his whole future ease, his very sureness of gait lay entirely in that money. It had become a tingling sensation for him, a smell, a feeling, a taste – $91,000 cash money in his safe at home. He had even stopped bothering to read the papers in the past year. Nothing that happened in the world could touch him while he had $91,000 in his closet.

There were three policemen sitting in the room when he entered. He identified himself, and they asked him to sit down. One of them went out. The remaining two were in shirt-sleeves and seemed to be merely waiting around. In a little while a grey-haired man entered, followed by a detective who carried a cheap canvas zipper bag which he set on a desk near the door. The detective introduced himself to Shelton, and asked him to repeat his description of the jewellery. Shelton did so in some detail, answering more specific questions as they occurred to the detective.

The grey-haired man had slumped into a chair. Now he sat staring at the floor. Shelton slowly realized, as he described the jewellery, that this was the thief; for the man seemed resigned, very tired, and completely at home in the situation.

The detective went at last to the desk and opened the zipper bag and laid out the jewellery for Shelton to inspect. Shelton glanced at it and said that it was his, picking up a wedding ring which had his name and his wife's name engraved on the inside.

'We'll have the coat for you by tomorrow and maybe the silver, too,' the detective said, idly arranging the jewellery in a pattern on the desk as he spoke. Shelton felt that the detective was getting at something from the way he played with the jewellery. The detective completed the pattern on the desk and then turned his broad, dark face toward Shelton and said, 'Is there anything else you lost?'

Shelton's hand, of its own accord, moved towards his heart as he said, 'That's all I can remember.'

The detective turned his whole body now and sat easily on the edge of the desk. 'You didn't lose any money?'

The grey-haired thief raised his head, a mystified look clouding his face.

'Money?' asked Shelton. And yet he could not help adding, 'What money?' just curiously.

'We found this on him,' the detective said, reaching into the bag and taking out five rolled-up wads of money wrapped in red rubber bands. Shelton's heart hurt him when he saw the rubber bands, because they, more than any of the other items, were peculiarly his. They were the rubber bands he always used in his office.

'There's $91,000 here,' the detective said.

The thief was looking up at Shelton from his chair, an expression of wounded bewilderment drawing his brows together. The detective merely sat on the desk, an observer; the moment suddenly belonged only to Shelton and the thief.

Shelton stared at the money without any expression on his face. It was too late to think fast; he had no idea what sort of mind this stolid detective had and he dared not hesitate long enough to sound the man out. A detective, Shelton knew, is higher than a cop; is more like a businessman, knows more. This one looks smart, and yet maybe. . . .

Shelton broke into a smile and touched one of the wads of bills that lay on the desk. (Oh, the $91,000; oh, the touch of it!) Sweat was running down his back; his heart pained like a wound. He smile and stalled for time. 'That's a lot of money,' he said softly, frantically studying the detective's eyes for a sign.

But the detective was impassive, and said, 'Is it yours?'

'Mine?' Shelton said, with a weak laugh. Longingly, he looked at the solid wads. 'I wish it were, but it isn't. I don't keep 91 thou –'

The thief, a tall man, stood up quickly and pointed to the money. 'What the hell is *this*?' he shouted, amazed.

The detective moved towards him, and he sat down again. 'It's his. I took it out of the safe with the other stuff.'

'Take it easy,' the detective said.

'Where did I get it, then?' the thief demanded in a more frightened tone. 'What're you trying to do, pin another job on me? I only pulled one, that's all! You asked me and I told you.' And, pointing directly up at Shelton's face, he said, 'He's pullin' something!'

The detective, as he turned to Shelton, was an agonizingly expressionless man who seemed to have neither pulse nor point of view. He simply stood there, the law with two little black eyes. 'You're sure,' he said, 'that this is not your money?'

'I ought to know,' Shelton said, laughing calmly.

The detective seemed to catch the absurdity of it, and very nearly smiled. Then he turned to the thief and, with a nod of his head, motioned him outside. The two policemen walked out behind him.

They were alone. The detective, without a word, returned to the desk and put the jewellery back into the zipper bag. Without turning his head, he said that they would return the stuff to Shelton in the morning. And then he picked up one of the heavy wads, but instead of dropping it into the bag he hefted it thoughtfully in his palm and turned his head to Shelton. 'Lot of dough,' he said.

'I'll say,' Shelton agreed.

The detective continued placing the wads in the bag. Shelton stood a little behind him and to one side, watching as best he could for the slightest change in the man's expression. But there was none; the detective might have been asleep but for his open eyes. Shelton wanted to leave – immediately. It was impossible to know what was happening in the detective's head.

And yet Shelton dared not indicate his desperation. He smiled again, and shifted his weight easily to one foot and started to button his coat, and said – as if the question was quite academic – 'What do you fellas do with money like that?'

The detective zipped the bag shut. 'Money like what?' he asked evenly.

A twinge of pain shot through Shelton's chest at the suspicious reserve in the detective's question. 'I mean, money that's not claimed,' he amended.

The detective walked past him toward the door. 'We wait,' he said and opened the door.

'I mean, supposing it's never claimed?' Shelton asked,

following him, still smiling as though with idle curiosity.

'Hot money is never claimed,' the detective said. 'We'll just wait. Then we'll start looking around.'

'I see.'

Shelton walked with the detective to the door of the precinct station, and he even talked amiably, and then they said a pleasant good night.

Staring at the pavement rolling under the wheels of his car, he could summon neither feeling nor thought. It was only when he opened the door of his house, the house which had once contained the fortune of his life, that his numbness flowed away, and he felt weak and ill.

'There must be a way to get it back,' she began.

'How?'

'You mean to tell me – ?'

'I mean to tell you!' he shouted, and got to his feet. 'What'll I do, break into the station house?'

'But they've got laws against robbery!'

In reply, Shelton pushed his collar open and climbed the stairs and went to bed.

These days, Shelton rides to business very slowly. The few friends he has on the block have grown accustomed to the grey and haunted stare in his eyes. The children seem to quiet down as he guides his car through their street games.

Sometimes he goes by the police station, and passing it he slows down and peers through the car window at it, but always goes on.

And when a police car rolls into the block on its ordinary tour, people can be seen stopping to watch until it passes his house. Nobody has said anything, of course, but we are waiting with Shelton for that awful moment when the police car pulls up at his door. And it must, of course.

Thirty days, maybe two months from now, it will turn the corner and slow down, and gradually, ominously, come to a stop.

The house is very quiet these nights – almost silent. The shades are drawn, and it is seldom that you see anyone going in or out. The Sheltons are waiting.

Goodbye, Pops

Joe Gores

I got off the Greyhound and stopped to draw icy Minnesota air into my lungs. A bus had brought me from Springfield, Illinois, to Chicago the day before; a second bus had brought me here. I caught my passing reflection in the window of the old-fashioned depot – a tall hard man with a white and savage face, wearing an ill-fitting overcoat. I caught another reflection, too, one that froze my guts: a cop in uniform. Could they already know it was actually someone else in the burned-out car?

Then the cop turned away, chafing his arms with gloved hands through his blue stormcoat, and I started breathing again. I went quickly over to the cab line. Only two hackies were waiting there; the front one rolled down his window as I came up.

'You know the Miller place north of town?' I asked. He looked me over. 'I know it. Five bucks – now.'

I paid him from the money I'd rolled a drunk for in Chicago and eased back against the rear seat. As he nursed the cab out of ice-rimed Second Street, my fingers gradually relaxed from their rigid chopping position. I deserved to go back inside if I let a clown like this get to me.

'Old man Miller's pretty sick, I hear.' He half turned to catch me with a corner of an eye. 'You got business with him?'

'Yeah. My own.'

That ended that conversation. It bothered me that Pops was sick enough for this clown to know about it; but maybe my brother Rod being vice-president at the bank would explain that. There was a lot of new construction and a freeway west of town with a tricky overpass to the old county road. A mile beyond a new sub-division were the 200 wooded hilly acres I knew so well.

After my break from the Federal pen at Terre Haute, Indiana, two days before, I'd gotten outside their cordon through woods like these. I'd gone out in a prison truck, in a pail of swill meant for the prison farm pigs, had headed straight west, across the Illinois line. I'm good in open country, even when I'm in prison condition, so by dawn I was in a hayloft near Paris, Illinois, some twenty miles from the pen. You can do what you have to do.

The cabby stopped at the foot of the private road, looking dubious. 'Listen, buddy, I know that's been ploughed, but it looks damned icy. If I try it and go into the ditch –'

'I'll walk from here.'

I waited beside the road until he'd driven away, then let the north wind chase me up the hill and into the leafless hardwoods. The cedars that Pops and I had put in as a windbreak were taller and fuller; rabbit paths were pounded hard into the snow under the barbed-wire tangles of wild raspberry bushes. Under the oaks at the top of the hill was the old-fashioned, two-storey house, but I detoured to the kennels first. The snow was deep and undisturbed inside them. No more foxhounds. No cracked corn in the bird feeder outside the kitchen window, either. I rang the front doorbell.

My sister-in-law Edwina, Rod's wife, answered it. She was three years younger than my 35, and she'd started wearing a girdle.

'Good Lord! Chris!' Her mouth tightened. 'We didn't –'

'Ma wrote that the old man was sick.' She'd written, all right. *Your father is very ill. Not that you have ever cared if any of us lives or dies. . . .* And then Edwina decided that my tone of voice had given her something to get righteous about.

'I'm amazed you'd have the nerve to come here, even if they did let you out on parole or something.' So nobody had been around asking yet. 'If you plan to drag the family name through the mud again –'

I pushed by her into the hallway. 'What's wrong with the old man?' I called him Pops only inside myself, where no one could hear.

'He's dying, that's what's wrong with him.'

She said it with a sort of baleful pleasure. It hit me, but I just grunted and went by into the living room. Then the old girl called down from the head of the stairs.

'Eddy? What – who is it?'

'Just – a salesman, Ma. He can wait until Doctor's gone.'

Doctor. As if some damned croaker was generic physician all by himself. When he came downstairs Edwina tried to hustle him out before I could see him, but I caught his arm as he poked it into his overcoat sleeve.

'Like to see you a minute, Doc. About old man Miller.'

He was nearly six feet, a couple of inches shorter than me, but outweighing me forty pounds. He pulled his arm free.

'Now, see here, fellow –'

I grabbed his lapels and shook him, just enough to pop a button off his coat and put his glasses awry on his nose. His face got red.

'Old family friend, Doc.' I jerked a thumb at the stairs. 'What's the story?'

It was dumb, dumb as hell, of course, asking him; at any second the cops would figure out that the farmer in the burned-out car wasn't me after all. I'd dumped enough gasoline before I struck the match so they couldn't lift prints off anything except the shoe I'd planted; but they'd make him through dental charts as soon as they found out he was missing. When they did they'd come here asking questions, and then the croaker would realize who I was. But I wanted to know whether Pops was as bad off as Edwina said he was, and I've never been a patient man.

The croaker straightened his suitcoat, striving to regain lost dignity. 'He – Judge Miller is very weak, too weak to move. He probably won't last out the week.' His eyes searched my face for pain, but there's nothing like a Federal pen to give you control. Disappointed, he said,

'His lungs. I got to it much too late, of course. He's resting easily.'

I jerked the thumb again. 'You know your way out.'

Edwina was at the head of the stairs, her face righteous again. It seems to run in the family, even with those who married in. Only Pops and I were short of it.

'Your father is very ill. I forbid you –'

'Save it for Rod; it might work on him.'

In the room I could see the old man's arm hanging limply over the edge of the bed, with smoke from the cigarette between his fingers running up to the ceiling in a thin unwavering blue line. The upper arm, which once had measured an honest 18 and had swung his small tight fist against the side of my head a score of times, could not even hold a cigarette up in the air. It gave me the same wrench as finding a good foxhound that's gotten mixed up with a bobcat.

The old girl came out of her chair by the foot of the bed, her face blanched. I put my arms around her. 'Hi, Ma,' I said. She was rigid inside my embrace, but I knew she wouldn't pull away. Not there in Pops's room.

He had turned his head at my voice. The light glinted from his silky white hair. His eyes, translucent with imminent death, were the pure, pale blue of birch shadows on fresh snow.

'Chris,' he said in a weak voice. 'Son of a biscuit, boy ... I'm glad to see you.'

'You ought to be, you lazy devil,' I said heartily. I pulled off my suit jacket and hung it over the back of the chair, and tugged off my tie. 'Getting so lazy that you let the foxhounds go!'

'That's enough, Chris.' She tried to put steel into it.

'I'll just sit here a little, Ma,' I said easily. Pops wouldn't have long, I knew, and any time I got with him would have to do me. She stood in the doorway, a dark indecisive shape; then she turned and went silently out, probably to phone Rod at the bank.

For the next couple of hours I did most of the talking; Pops just lay there with his eyes shut, like he was asleep. But then he started in, going way back, to the trapline he and I had run when I'd been a kid; to the big white-tail buck that followed him through the woods one rutting season until Pops whacked it on the nose with a tree branch. It was only after his law practice had ripened into a judgeship that we began to draw apart; I guess that in my twenties I was too wild, too much what he'd been himself 30 years before. Only I kept going in that direction.

About seven o'clock my brother Rod called from the doorway. I went out, shutting the door behind me. Rod was taller than me, broad and big-boned, with an athlete's frame – but with mush where his guts should have been. He had close-set pale eyes and not quite enough chin, and hadn't gone out for football in high school.

'My wife reported the vicious things you said to her.' It was his best give-the-teller-hell voice. 'We've talked this over with mother and we want you out of here tonight. We want –'

'*You* want? Until he kicks off it's still the old man's house, isn't it?'

He swung at me then – being Rod, it was a right-hand lead – and I blocked it with an open palm. Then I backhanded him, hard, twice across the face each way, jerking his head from side to side with the slaps, and crowding him against the wall. I could have fouled his groin to bend him over, then driven locked hands down on the back of his neck as I jerked a knee into his face; and I wanted to. The need to get away before they came after me was gnawing at my gut like a weasel in a trap gnawing off his own paw to get loose. But I merely stepped away from him.

'You – you murderous animal!' He had both his hands up to his cheeks like a woman might have done. Then his eyes widened theatrically, as the realization struck him. I wondered why it had taken so long. 'You've *broken out!*' he gasped. '*Escaped!* A fugitive from – from justice!'

'Yeah. And I'm staying that way. I know you, kid, all of you. The last thing any of you want is for the cops to take me here.' I tried to put his tones into my voice. '*Oh!* The *scandal!*'

'But they'll be after you –'

'They think I'm dead,' I said flatly. 'I went off an icy

road in a stolen car in down-state Illinois, and it rolled and burned with me inside.'

His voice was hushed, almost horror-stricken. 'You mean – that there *is* a body in the car?'

'Right.'

I knew what he was thinking, but I didn't bother to tell him the truth – that the old farmer who was driving me to Springfield, because he thought my doubled-up fist in the overcoat pocket was a gun, hit a patch of ice and took the car right off the lonely country road. He was impaled on the steering post, so I took his shoes and put one of mine on his foot. The other I left, with my fingerprints on it, lying near enough so they'd find it, but not so near that it'd burn along with the car. Rod wouldn't have believed the truth anyway. If they caught me, who would?

I said, 'Bring me up a bottle of bourbon and a carton of cigarettes. And make sure Eddy and Ma keep their mouths shut if anyone asks about me.' I opened the door so Pops could hear. 'Well, thanks, Rod. It is nice to be home again.'

Solitary in the pen makes you able to stay awake easily or snatch sleep easily, whichever is necessary. I stayed awake for the last 37 hours that Pops had, leaving the chair by his bed only to go to the bathroom and to listen at the head of the stairs whenever I heard the phone or the doorbell ring. Each time I thought: *this is it.* But my luck held. If they'd just take long enough so I could stay until Pops went; the second that happened, I told myself, I'd be on my way.

Rod and Edwina and Ma were at the end, with Doctor hovering in the background to make sure he got paid. Pops finally moved a pallid arm, and Ma sat down quickly on the edge of the bed – a small, erect, rather indomitable woman with a face made for wearing a lorgnette. She wasn't crying yet; instead, she looked purely luminous in a way.

'Hold my hand, Eileen.' Pops paused for the terrible strength to speak again. 'Hold my hand. Then I won't be frightened.'

She took his hand and he almost smiled, and shut his eyes. We waited, listening to his breathing get slower and slower and then just stop, like a grandfather clock running down. Nobody moved, nobody spoke. I looked around at them, so soft, so unused to death, and I felt like a marten in a brooding house. Then Ma began to sob.

It was a blustery day with snow flurries. I parked the jeep in front of the funeral chapel and went up the slippery walk with wind plucking at my coat, telling myself for the hundredth time just how nuts I was to stay for the service. By now they *had* to know that the dead farmer wasn't me; by now some smart prison censor *had* to remember Ma's letter about Pops being sick. He was two days dead, and I should have been in Mexico by this time. But it didn't seem complete yet, somehow. Or maybe I was kidding myself, maybe it was just the old need to put down authority that always ruins guys like me.

From a distance it looked like Pops but up close you could see the cosmetics and that his collar was three sizes too big. I felt his hand: it was a statue's hand, unfamiliar except for the thick, slightly down-curved fingernails.

Rod came up behind me and said, in a voice meant only for me, 'After today I want you to leave us alone. I want you out of my house.'

'Shame on you, brother,' I grinned. 'Before the will is even read, too.'

We followed the hearse through snowy streets at the proper funeral pace, lights burning. Pallbearers wheeled the heavy casket out smoothly on oiled tracks, then set it on belts over the open grave. Snow whipped and swirled from a gray sky, melting on the metal and forming rivulets down the sides.

I left when the preacher started his scam, impelled by the need to get moving, get away, yet impelled by another urgency, too. I wanted something out of the house before all the mourners arrived to eat and guzzle. The guns and ammo already had been banished to the garage, since Rod never had fired a round in his life; but it was easy to dig out the beautiful little .22 target pistol with the long barrel. Pops and I had spent hundreds of hours with that gun, so the grip was worn smooth and the blueing was gone from the metal that had been out in every sort of weather.

Putting the jeep on four-wheel, I ran down through the trees to a cut between the hills, then went along on foot through the darkening hardwoods. I moved slowly, evoking memories of Korea to neutralize the icy bite of the snow through my worn shoes. There was a flash of brown as a cottontail streaked from under a deadfall toward a rotting woodpile I'd stacked years before. My slug took him in the spine, paralysing the back legs. He jerked and thrashed until I broke his neck with the edge of my hand.

I left him there and moved out again, down into the small marshy triangle between the hills. It was darkening fast as I kicked at the frozen tussocks. Finally a ringneck in full plumage burst out, long tail fluttering and stubby pheasant wings beating to raise his heavy body. He was quartering up and just a bit to my right, and I had all the time in the world. I squeezed off in mid-wing, knowing it was perfect even before he took that heart-stopping pinwheel tumble.

I carried them back to the jeep; there was a tiny ruby of blood on the pheasant's beak, and the rabbit was still hot under the front legs. I was using headlights when I parked on the curving cemetery drive. They hadn't put the casket down yet, so the snow had laid a soft blanket over it. I put the rabbit and pheasant on top and stood without moving for a minute or two. The wind must have been strong, because I found that tears were burning on my cheeks.

Goodbye, Pops. Goodbye to deer-shining out of season in the hardwood belt across the creek. Goodbye to jump-shooting mallards down in the river bottoms. Goodbye to woodsmoke and mellow bourbon by firelight and all the things that made a part of you mine. The part they could never get at.

I turned away, toward the jeep – and stopped dead. I hadn't even heard them come up. Four of them, waiting patiently as if to pay their respects to the dead. In one sense they were: to them that dead farmer in the burned-out car was Murder One. I tensed, my mind going to the .22 pistol that they didn't know about in my overcoat pocket. Yeah. Except that it had all the stopping power of a fox's bark. If only Pops had run to guns of a little heavier calibre. But he hadn't.

Very slowly, as if my arms suddenly had grown very heavy, I raised my hands above my head.

The Best-Friend Murder

Donald E. Westlake

Detective Abraham Levine of Brooklyn's Forty-Third Precinct chewed on his pencil and glowered at the report he'd just written. He didn't like it, he didn't like it at all. It just didn't feel right, and the more he thought about it the stronger the feeling became.

Levine was a short and stocky man, baggily-dressed from plain pipe racks. His face was sensitive, topped by salt-and-pepper grey hair chopped short in a military crewcut. At fifty-three, he had twenty-four years of duty on the police force, and was halfway through the heart-attack age range, a fact that had been bothering him for some time now. Every time he was reminded of death, he thought worriedly about the aging heart pumping away inside his chest.

And in his job, the reminders of death came often. Natural death, accidental death, and violent death.

This one was a violent death, and to Levine it felt wrong somewhere. He and his partner, Jack Crawley, had taken the call just after lunch. It was from one of the patrolmen in Prospect Park, a patrolman named Tanner. A man giving his name as Larry Perkins had walked up to Tanner in the park and announced that he had just poisoned his best friend. Tanner went with him, found a dead body in the apartment Perkins had led him to, and called in. Levine and Crawley, having just walked into the station after lunch, were given the call. They turned around and walked back out again.

Crawley drove their car, an unmarked '56 Chevy, while Levine sat beside him and worried about death. At least this would be one of the neat ones. No knives or bombs or broken beer bottles. Just poison, that was all. The victim would look as though he were sleeping, unless it had been one of those poisons causing muscle spasms before death. But it would still be neater than a knife or a bomb or a broken beer bottle, and the victim wouldn't look quite so completely dead.

Crawley drove leisurely, without the siren. He was a big man in his forties, somewhat overweight, square-faced and heavy-jowled, and he looked meaner than he actually was. The Chevy tooled up Eighth Avenue, the late spring sun shining on its hood. They were headed for an address on Garfield Place, the block between Eighth Avenue and Prospect Park West. They had to circle the block, because Garfield was a one-way street. That particular block on Garfield Place is a double row of chipped brownstones, the street running down between two rows of high stone stoops, the buildings cut and chopped inside into thousands of apartments, crannies and cubbyholes, niches and box-like caves, where the subway riders sleep at night. The subway to Manhattan is six blocks away, up at Grand Army Plaza, across the way from the main library.

At one p.m. on this Wednesday in late May, the sidewalks were deserted, the buildings had the look of long abandoned dwellings. Only the cars parked along the left side of the street indicated present occupancy.

The number they wanted was in the middle of the block, on the right-hand side. There was no parking allowed on that side, so there was room directly in front of the address for Crawley to stop the Chevy. He flipped the sun visor down, with the official business card showing through the windshield, and followed Levine across the sidewalk and down the two steps to the basement door, under the stoop. The door was propped open with a battered garbage can. Levine and Crawley walked inside. It was dim in there, after the bright sunlight, and it took Levine's eyes a few seconds to get used to the change. Then he made out the figures of two men standing at the other end of the hallway, in front of a closed door. One was the patrolman, Tanner, young, just over six feet, with a square and impersonal face. The other was Larry Perkins.

Levine and Crawley moved down the hallway to the

two men waiting for them. In the seven years they had been partners, they had established a division of labour that satisfied them both. Crawley asked the questions, and Levine listened to the answers. Now, Crawley introduced himself to Tanner, who said, 'This is Larry Perkins of 294 Fourth Street.'

'Body in there?' asked Crawley, pointing at the closed door.

'Yes, sir,' said Tanner.

'Let's go inside,' said Crawley. 'You keep an eye on the pigeon. See he doesn't fly away.'

'I've got some stuff to go to the library,' said Perkins suddenly. His voice was young and soft.

They stared at him. Crawley said, 'It'll keep.'

Levine looked at Perkins, trying to get to know him. It was a technique he used, most of it unconsciously. First, he tried to fit Perkins into a type or category, some sort of general stereotype. Then he would look for small and individual ways in which Perkins differed from the general type, and he would probably wind up with a surprisingly complete mental picture, which would also be surprisingly accurate.

The general stereotype was easy, Perkins, in his black wool sweater and belt-in-the-back khakis and scuffed brown loafers without socks, was 'arty.' What were they calling them this year? They were 'hip' last year, but this year they were – 'beat.' That was it. For a general stereotype, Larry Perkins was a Beatnik. The individual differences would show up soon, in Perkins' talk and mannerisms and attitudes.

Crawley said again, 'Let's go inside,' and the four of them trooped into the room where the corpse lay.

The apartment was one large room, plus a closet-size kitchenette and an even smaller bathroom. A Murphy bed stood open, covered with zebra-striped material. The rest of the furniture consisted of a battered dresser, a couple of armchairs and lamps, and a record player sitting on a table beside a huge stack of long-playing records. Everything except the record player looked faded and worn and second-hand, including the thin maroon rug on the floor and the soiled flower-pattern wallpaper. Two windows looked out on a narrow cement enclosure and the back of another brownstone. It was a sunny day outside, but no sun managed to get down into this room.

In the middle of the room stood a card table, with a typewriter and two stacks of paper on it. Before the card table was a folding chair, and in the chair sat the dead man. He was slumped forward, his arms flung out and crumpling the stacks of paper, his head resting on the typewriter. His face was turned toward the door, and his eyes were closed, his facial muscles relaxed. It had been a peaceful death, at least, and Levine was grateful for that.

Crawley looked at the body, grunted, and turned to Perkins. 'Okay,' he said. 'Tell us about it.'

'I put the poison in his beer,' said Perkins simply. He didn't talk like a Beatnik at any rate. 'He asked me to open a can of beer for him. When I poured it into a glass, I put the poison in, too. When he was dead, I went and talked to the patrolman here.'

'And that's all there was to it?'

'That's all.'

Levine asked, 'Why did you kill him?'

Perkins looked over at Levine. 'Because he was a pompous ass.'

'Look at me,' Crawley told him.

Perkins immediately looked away from Levine, but before he did so, Levine caught a flicker of emotion in the boy's eyes, what emotion he couldn't tell. Levine glanced around the room, at the faded furniture and the card table and the body, and at young Perkins, dressed like a Beatnik but talking like the politest of polite young men, outwardly calm but hiding some strong emotion deep inside his eyes. What was it Levine had seen there? Terror? Rage? Or pleading?

'Tell us about this guy,' said Crawley, motioning at the body. 'His name, where you knew him from, the whole thing.'

'His name is Al Gruber. He got out of the Army about eight months ago. He's living on his savings and the GI Bill. I mean, he *was*.'

'He was a college student?'

'More or less. He was taking a few courses at Columbia, nights. He wasn't a full-time student?'

Crawley said, 'What was he, full-time?'

Perkins shrugged. 'Not much of anything. A writer. An undiscovered writer. Like me.'

Levine asked, 'Did he make much money from his writing?'

'None,' said Perkins. This time he didn't turn to look at Levine, but kept watching Crawley while he answered. 'He got something accepted by one of the quarterlies once,' he said, 'but I don't think they ever published it. And they don't pay anything anyway.'

'So he was broke?' asked Crawley.

'Very broke. I know the feeling well.'

'You in the same boat?'

'Same life story completely,' said Perkins. He glanced at the body of Al Gruber and said, 'Well, almost. I write, too. And I don't get any money for it. And I'm living on the GI Bill and savings and a few home-typing jobs, and going to Columbia nights.'

People came into the room then, the medical examiner and the boys from the lab, and Levine and Crawley, bracketing Perkins between them, waited and watched for a while. When they could see that the M.E. had completed his first examination, they left Perkins in Tanner's charge and went over to talk to him.

Crawley, as usual, asked the questions. 'Hi, Doc,' he said. 'What's it look like to you?'

'Pretty straightforward case,' said the M.E. 'On the surface, anyway. Our man here was poisoned, felt the effects coming on, went to the typewriter to tell us who'd done it to him, and died. A used glass and a small medicine bottle were on the dresser. We'll check them out, but they almost certainly did the job.'

'Did he manage to do any typing before he died?' asked Crawley.

The M.E. shook his head. 'Not a word. The paper was in the machine kind of crooked, as though he'd been in a hurry, but he just wasn't fast enough.'

'He wasted his time,' said Crawley. 'The guy confessed right away.'

'The one over there with the patrolman?'

'Uh-huh.'

'Seems odd, doesn't it?' said the M.E. 'Take the trouble to poison someone, and then run out and confess to the first cop you see.'

Crawley shrugged. 'You can never figure,' he said.

'I'll get the report to you soon's I can,' said the M.E.

'Thanks, Doc. Come on, Abe, let's take our pigeon to his nest.'

'Okay,' said Levine, abstractedly. Already it felt wrong. It had been feeling wrong, vaguely, ever since he'd caught that glimpse of something in Perkins' eyes. And the feeling of wrongness was getting stronger by the minute, without getting any clearer.

They walked back to Tanner.

'You're going to book me?' asked Perkins. He sounded oddly eager.

'Just come along,' said Crawley. He didn't believe in answering extraneous questions.

'All right,' said Perkins. He turned to Tanner. 'Would you mind taking my books and records back to the library? They're due today. They're the ones on the chair. And there's a couple more in the stack of Al's records.'

'Sure,' said Tanner. He was gazing at Perkins with a troubled look on his face, and Levine wondered if Tanner felt the same wrongness that was plaguing him.

'Let's go,' said Crawley impatiently, and Perkins moved toward the door.

'I'll be right along,' said Levine. As Crawley and Perkins left the apartment, Levine glanced at the titles of the books and record albums Perkins had wanted returned to the library. Two of the books were collections of Elizabethan plays, one was the *New Arts Writing Annual*, and the other two were books on criminology. The records were mainly folk songs, of the bloodier type.

Levine frowned and went over to Tanner. He asked, 'What were you and Perkins talking about before we got here?'

Tanner's face was still creased in a puzzled frown. 'The stupidity of the criminal mind,' he said. 'There's something goofy here, Lieutenant.'

'You may be right,' Levine told him. He walked on down the hall and joined the other two at the door.

All three got into the front seat of the Chevy, Crawley driving again and Perkins sitting in the middle. They rode in silence, Crawley busy driving, Perkins studying the complex array of the dashboard, with its extra knobs and switches and the mike hooked beneath the radio, and Levine trying to figure out what was wrong.

At the station, after booking, they brought him to a small office, one of the interrogation rooms. There was a bare and battered desk, plus four chairs. Crawley sat behind the desk, Perkins sat across the desk and facing him, Levine took the chair in a corner behind and to the left of Perkins, and a male stenographer, notebook in hand, filled the fourth chair, behind Crawley.

Crawley's first questions covered the same ground already covered at Gruber's apartment, this time for the record. 'Okay,' said Crawley, when he'd brought them up to date. 'You and Gruber were both doing the same kind of thing, living the same kind of life. You were both unpublished writers, both taking night courses at Columbia, both living on very little money.'

'That's right,' said Perkins.

'How long you known each other?'

'About six months. We met at Columbia, and we took the same subway home after class. We got to talking, found out we were both dreaming the same kind of dream, and became friends. You know. Misery loves company.'

'Take the same classes at Columbia?'

'Only one. Creative Writing, from Professor Stonegell.'

'Where'd you buy the poison?'

'I didn't. Al did. He bought it a while back and just kept it around. He kept saying if he didn't make a good sale soon he'd kill himself. But he didn't mean it. It was just a kind of gag.'

Crawley pulled at his right ear lobe. Levine knew, from his long experience with his partner, that that gesture meant that Crawley was confused. 'You went there today to kill him?'

'That's right.'

Levine shook his head. That wasn't right. Softly, he said, 'Why did you bring the library books along?'

'I was on my way up to the library,' said Perkins, twisting around in his seat to look at Levine.

'Look this way,' snapped Crawley.

Perkins looked around at Crawley again, but not before Levine had seen that same burning deep in Perkins' eyes. Stronger, this time, and more like pleading. Pleading? What was Perkins pleading for?

'I was on my way to the library,' Perkins said again. 'Al had a couple of records out on my card, so I went over to get them. On the way, I decided to kill him.'

'Why?' asked Crawley.

'Because he was a pompous ass,' said Perkins, the same answer he'd given before.

'Because he got a story accepted by one of the literary magazines and you didn't?' suggested Crawley.

'Maybe. Partially. His whole attitude. He was smug. He knew more than anybody else in the world.'

'Why did you kill him today? Why not last week or next week?'

'I felt like it today.'

'Why did you give yourself up?'

'You would have gotten me anyway.'

Levine asked, 'Did you know that before you killed him?'

'I don't know,' said Perkins, without looking around at Levine. 'I didn't think about it till afterward. Then I knew the police would get me anyway – they'd talk to Professor Stonegell and the other people who knew us both and I didn't want to have to wait it out. So I went and confessed.'

'You told the patrolman,' said Levine, 'that you killed your best friend.'

'That's right.'

'Why did you use that phrase, best friend, if you hated him so much you wanted to kill him?'

'He was my best friend. At least, in New York. I didn't really know anyone else, except Professor Stonegell. Al was my best friend because he was just about my only friend.'

'Are you sorry you killed him?' asked Levine.

This time, Perkins twisted around in the chair again, ignoring Crawley. 'No, sir,' he said, and his eyes now were blank.

There was silence in the room, and Crawley and Levine looked at one another. Crawley questioned with his eyes, and Levine shrugged, shaking his head. Something was wrong, but he didn't know what. And Perkins was being so helpful that he wound up being no help at all.

Crawley turned to the stenographer. 'Type it up formal,' he said. 'And have somebody come to take the pigeon to his nest.'

After the stenographer had left, Levine said, 'Anything you want to say off the record, Perkins?'

Perkins grinned. His face was half-turned away from Crawley, and he was looking at the floor, as though he was amused by something he saw there. 'Off the record?' he murmured. 'As long as there are two of you in here, it's *on* the record.'

'Do you want one of us to leave?'

Perkins looked up at Levine again, and stopped smiling. He seemed to think it over for a minute, and then he shook his head. 'No,' he said. 'Thanks, anyway. But I don't think I have anything more to say. Not right now anyway.'

Levine frowned and sat back in his chair, studying Perkins. The boy didn't ring true; he was constructed of too many contradictions. Levine reached out for a mental image of Perkins, but all he touched was air.

After Perkins was led out of the room by two uniformed cops, Crawley got to his feet, stretched, sighed, scratched, pulled his earlobe, and said, 'What do you make of it, Abe?'

'I don't like it.'

'I know that. I saw it in your face. But he confessed, so what else is there?'

'The phoney confession is not exactly unheard of, you know.'

'Not this time,' said Crawley. 'A guy confesses to a crime he didn't commit for one of two reasons. Either he's a crackpot who wants the publicity or to be punished or something like that, or he's protecting somebody else. Perkins doesn't read like a crackpot to me, and there's nobody else involved for him to be protecting.'

'In a capital punishment state,' suggested Levine, 'a guy might confess to a murder he didn't commit so the state would do his suicide for him.'

Crawley shook his head. 'That still doesn't look like Perkins,' he said.

'Nothing looks like Perkins. He's given us a blank wall to stare at. A couple of times it started to slip, and there was something else inside.'

'Don't build a big thing, Abe. The kid confessed. He's the killer; let it go at that.'

'The job's finished, I know that. But it still bothers me.'

'Okay,' said Crawley. He sat down behind the desk again and put his feet up on the scarred desk top. 'Let's straighten it out. Where does it bother you?'

'All over. Number one, motivation. You don't kill a man for being a pompous ass. Not when you turn around a minute later and say he was your best friend.'

'People do funny things when they're pushed far enough. Even to friends.'

'Sure. Okay, number two. The murder method. It doesn't sound right. When a man kills impulsively, he grabs something and starts swinging. When he calms down, he goes and turns himself in. But when you *poison* somebody, you're using a pretty sneaky method. It doesn't make sense for you to run out and call a cop right after using poison. It isn't the same kind of mentality.'

'He used the poison,' said Crawley, 'because it was handy. Gruber bought it, probably had it sitting on his dresser or something, and Perkins just picked it up on impulse and poured it into the beer.'

'That's another thing,' said Levine. 'Do you drink much beer out of cans?'

Crawley grinned. 'You know I do.'

'I saw some empty beer cans sitting around the apartment, so that's where Gruber got his last beer from.'

'Yeah. So what?'

‘When you drink a can of beer, do you pour the beer out of the can into a glass, or do you just drink it straight from the can?’

‘I drink it out of the can. But not everybody does.’

‘I know, I know. Okay, what about the library books? If you’re going to kill somebody, are you going to bring library books along?’

‘It was an impulse killing. He didn’t know he was going to do it until he got there.’

Levine got to his feet. ‘That’s the hell of it,’ he said. ‘You can explain away every single question in this business. But it’s such a simple case. Why should there be so many questions that need explaining away?’

Crawley shrugged. ‘Beats me,’ he said. ‘All I know is, we’ve got a confession, and that’s enough to satisfy me.’

‘Not me,’ said Levine. ‘I think I’ll go poke around and see what happens. Want to come along?’

‘Somebody’s going to have to hand the pen to Perkins when he signs his confession,’ said Crawley.

‘Mind if I take off for a while?’

‘Go ahead. Have a big time,’ said Crawley, grinning at him. ‘Play detective.’

Levine’s first stop was back at Gruber’s address. Gruber’s apartment was empty now, having been sifted completely through normal routine procedure. Levine went down to the basement door under the stoop, but he didn’t go back to Gruber’s door. He stopped at the front apartment instead, where a ragged-edge strip of paper attached with peeling scotch tape to the door read, in awkward and childish lettering, SUPERINTENDENT. Levine rapped and waited. After a minute, the door opened a couple of inches, held by a chain. A round face peered out at him from a height of a little over five feet, ‘Who you looking for?’

‘Police,’ Levine told him. He opened his wallet and held it up for the face to look at.

‘Oh,’ said the face. ‘Sure thing.’ The door shut, and Levine waited while the chain was clinked free, and then the door opened wide.

The super was a short and round man, dressed in corduroy trousers and a grease-spotted undershirt. He wheezed, 'Come in, come in,' and stood back for Levine to come into his crowded and musty-smelling living room.

Levine said, 'I want to talk to you about Al Gruber.'

The super shut the door and waddled into the middle of the room, shaking his head. 'Wasn't that a shame?' he asked. 'Al was a nice boy. No money, but a nice boy. Sit down somewhere, anywhere.'

Levine looked around. The room was full of low-slung, heavy, sagging, over-stuffed furniture, armchairs and sofas. He picked the least battered armchair of the lot, and sat on the very edge. Although he was a short man, his knees seemed to be almost up to his chin, and he had the feeling that if he relaxed he'd fall over backward.

The super trundled across the room and dropped into one of the other armchairs, sinking into it as though he never intended to get to his feet again in his life. 'A real shame,' he said again. 'And to think I maybe could have stopped it.'

'You could have stopped it? How?'

'It was around noon,' said the super. 'I was watching the TV over there, and I heard a voice from the back apartment, shouting, "Al! Al!" So I went out to the hall, but by the time I got there the shouting was all done. So I didn't know what to do. I waited a minute, and then I came back in and watched the TV again. That was probably when it was happening.'

'There wasn't any noise while you were in the hall? Just the two shouts before you got out there?'

'That's all. At first, I thought it was another of them arguments, and I was gonna bawl out the two of them, but it stopped before I even got the door open.'

'Arguments?'

'Mr Gruber and Mr Perkins. They used to argue all the time, shout at each other, carry on like monkeys. The other tenants was always complaining about it. They'd do it late at night sometimes, two or three o'clock in the morning, and the tenants would all start phoning me to complain.'

'What did they argue about?'

The super shrugged his massive shoulders. 'Who

knows? Names. People. Writers. They both think they're great writers or something.'

'Did they ever get into a fist fight or anything like that? Ever threaten to kill each other?'

'Naw, they'd just shout at each other and call each other stupid and ignorant and stuff like that. They liked each other, really, I guess. At least they always hung around together. They just loved to argue, that's all. You know how it is with college kids. I've had college kids renting here before, and they're all like that. They all love to argue. Course, I never had nothing like this happen before.'

'What kind of person was Gruber, exactly?'

The super mulled it over for a while. 'Kind of a quiet guy,' he said at last. 'Except when he was with Mr Perkins, I mean. Then he'd shout just as loud and often as anybody. But most of the time he was quiet. And good-mannered. A real surprise, after most of the kids around today. He was always polite, and he'd lend a hand if you needed some help or something, like the time I was carrying a bed up to the third floor front. Mr Gruber came along and pitched right in with me. He did more of the work than I did.'

'And he was a writer, wasn't he? At least, he was trying to be a writer.'

'Oh, sure. I'd hear that typewriter of his tappin' away in there at all hours. And he always carried a notebook around with him, writin' things down in it. I asked him once what he wrote in there, and he said descriptions, of places like Prospect Park up at the corner, and of the people he knew. He always said he wanted to be a writer like some guy named Wolfe, used to live in Brooklyn too.'

'I see.' Levine struggled out of the armchair. 'Thanks for your time,' he said.

'Not at all.' The super waddled after Levine to the door. 'Anything I can do,' he said. 'Any time at all.'

'Thanks again,' said Levine. He went outside and stood in the hallway, thinking things over, listening to the latch click in place behind him. Then he turned and walked down the hallway to Gruber's apartment, and knocked on the door.

As he'd expected, a uniformed cop had been left behind to keep an eye on the place for a while, and when he opened the door, Levine showed his identification and said, 'I'm on the case. I'd like to take a look around.'

The cop let him in, and Levine looked carefully through Gruber's personal property. He found the notebooks, finally, in the bottom drawer of the dresser. There were five of them, steno pad size loose-leaf fillers. Four of them were filled with writing, in pen, in a slow and careful hand, and the fifth was still half-blank.

Levine carried the notebooks over to the card table, pushed the typewriter out of the way, sat down and began to skim through the books.

He found what he was looking for in the middle of the third one he tried. A description of Larry Perkins, written by the man Perkins had killed. The description, or character study, which it more closely resembled, was four pages long, beginning with a physical description and moving into a discussion of Perkins' personality. Levine noticed particular sentences in this latter part: 'Larry doesn't want to write, he wants to be a writer, and that isn't the same thing. He wants the glamour and the fame and the money, and he thinks he'll get it from being a writer. That's why he's dabbled in acting and painting and all the other so-called glamorous professions. Larry and I are both being thwarted by the same thing; neither of us has anything to say worth saying. The difference is, I'm trying to find something to say, and Larry wants to make it on glibness alone. One of these days, he's going to find out he won't get anywhere that way. That's going to be a terrible day for him.'

Levine closed the book, then picked up the last one, the one that hadn't yet been filled, and leafed through that. One word kept showing up throughout the last notebook. 'Nihilism.' Gruber obviously hated the word, and he was also obviously afraid of it. 'Nihilism is death,' he wrote on one page. 'It is the belief that there are no beliefs, that no effort is worthwhile. How could any writer believe such a thing? Writing is the most positive of acts. So how can it be used for negative purposes? The only expression of nihilism is death, not the written word. If I can say nothing hopeful, I shouldn't say anything at all.'

Levine put the notebooks back in the dresser drawer finally, thanked the cop, and went out to the Chevy. He'd hoped to be able to fill in the blank spaces in Perkins' character through Gruber's notebooks, but Gruber had apparently had just as much trouble defining Perkins as Levine was now having. Levine had learned a lot about the dead man, that he was sincere and intense and self-demanding as only the young can be, but Perkins was still little more than a smooth and blank wall. 'Glibness,' Gruber had called it. What was beneath the glibness? A murderer, by Perkins' own admission. But what else?

Levine crawled wearily into the Chevy and headed for Manhattan.

Professor Harvey Stonegell was in class when Levine got to Columbia University, but the girl at the desk in the dean's outer office told him that Stonegell would be out of that class in just a few minutes and would then be free for the rest of the afternoon. She gave him directions to Stonegell's office, and Levine thanked her.

Stonegell's office door was locked, so Levine waited in the hall, watching the students hurrying by in both directions, and reading the notices of scholarships, grants and fellowships thumb-tacked to the bulletin board near the office door.

The professor showed up about fifteen minutes later, with two students in tow. He was a tall and slender man, with a gaunt face and a full head of grey-white hair. He could have been any age between fifty and seventy. He wore a tweed suit jacket, leather patches at the elbows, and non-matching grey slacks.

Levine said, 'Professor Stonegell?'

'Yes?'

Levine introduced himself and showed his identification. 'I'd like to talk to you for a minute or two.'

'Of course. I'll just be a minute.' Stonegell handed a book to one of the two students, telling him to read certain sections of it, and explained to the other student why he hadn't received a passing grade in his latest assignment. When both of them were taken care of, Levine stepped into Stonegell's crowded and tiny office, and sat down in the chair beside the desk.

Stonegell said, 'Is this about one of my students?'

'Two of them. From your evening writing course. Gruber and Perkins.'

'Those two? They aren't in trouble, are they?'

'I'm afraid so. Perkins has confessed to murdering Gruber.'

Stonegell's thin face paled. 'Gruber's dead? Murdered?'

'By Perkins. He turned himself in right after it happened. But, to be honest with you, the whole thing bothers me. It doesn't make sense. You knew them both. I thought you might be able to tell me something about them, so it *would* make sense.'

Stonegell lit himself a cigarette, offered one to Levine, but Levine declined. He'd given up cigarettes shortly after he'd started worrying about his heart.

'This takes some getting used to,' said Stonegell after a minute. 'Gruber and Perkins. They were both good students in my class, Gruber perhaps a bit better. And they were friends.'

'I'd heard they were friends.'

'There was a friendly rivalry between them,' said Stonegell. 'Whenever one of them started a project, the other one started a similar project, intent on beating the first one at his own game. Actually, that was more Perkins than Gruber. And they always took opposite sides of every question, screamed at each other like sworn enemies. But actually they were very close friends. I can't understand either one of them murdering the other.'

'Was Gruber similar to Perkins?'

'Did I give that impression? No, they were definitely unalike. The old business about opposites attracting. Gruber was by far the more sensitive and sincere of the two. I don't mean to imply that Perkins was insensitive or insincere at all. Perkins had his own sensitivity and his own sincerity, but they were almost exclusively directed within himself. He equated everything with himself, his own feelings and his own ambitions. But

Gruber had more of the – oh, I don't know – more of a *world-view*, to badly translate the German. His sensitivity was directed outward, toward the feelings of other people. It showed up in their writing. Gruber's forte was characterization, subtle interplay between personalities. Perkins was deft, almost glib, with movement and action and plot, but his characters lacked substance. He wasn't really interested in anyone but himself.'

'He doesn't sound like the kind of guy who'd confess to a murder right after he committed it.'

'I know what you mean. That isn't like him. I don't imagine Perkins would ever feel remorse or guilt. I should think he would be one of the people who believes the only crime is being caught.'

'Yet we didn't catch him. He came to us.' Levine studied the book titles on the shelf behind Stonegell. 'What about their mental attitudes recently?' he asked. 'Generally speaking, I mean. Were they happy or unhappy, impatient or content or what?'

'I think they were both rather depressed, actually,' said Stonegell. 'Though for somewhat different reasons. They had both come out of the Army less than a year ago, and had come to New York to try to make their mark as writers. Gruber was having difficulty with subject matter. We talked about it a few times. He couldn't find anything he really wanted to write about, nothing he felt strongly enough to give him direction in his writing.'

'And Perkins?'

'He wasn't particularly worried about writing in that way. He was as I say, deft and rather clever in his writing, but it was all too shallow. I think they might have been bad for one another, actually. Perkins could see that Gruber had the depth and sincerity that he lacked, and Gruber thought that Perkins was free from the soul-searching and self-doubt that was hampering him so much. In the last month or so, both of them have talked about dropping out of school, going back home and forgetting about the whole thing. But neither of them could have done that, at least not yet. Gruber couldn't have, because the desire to write was too strong in him.

Perkins couldn't, because the desire to be a famous writer was too strong.'

'A year seems like a pretty short time to get all that depressed,' said Levine.

Stonegell smiled. 'When you're young,' he said, 'a year can be eternity. Patience is an attribute of the old.'

'I suppose you're right. What about girl friends, other people who knew them both?'

'Well, there was one girl whom both were dating rather steadily. The rivalry again. I don't think either of them were particularly serious about her, but both of them wanted to take her away from the other one.'

'Do you know this girl's name?'

'Yes, of course. She was in the same class with Perkins and Gruber. I think I might have her home address here.'

Stonegell opened a small file drawer atop his desk, and looked through it. 'Yes, here it is,' he said. 'Her name is Anne Marie Stone, and she lives on Grove Street, down in the Village. Here you are.'

Levine accepted the card from Stonegell, copied the name and address onto his pad, and gave the card back. He got to his feet. 'Thank you for your trouble,' he said.

'Not at all,' said Stonegell, standing. He extended his hand, and Levine, shaking it, found it bony and almost parchment-thin, but surprisingly strong. 'I don't know if I've been much help, though,' he said.

'Neither do I, yet,' said Levine. 'I may be just wasting both our time. Perkins confessed, after all.'

'Still –' said Stonegell.

Levine nodded. 'I know. That's what's got me doing extra work.'

'I'm still thinking of this thing as though – as though it were a story problem, if you know what I mean. It isn't real yet. Two young students, I've taken an interest in both of them, fifty years after the worms get me they'll still be around – and then you tell me one of them is already wormfood, and the other one is effectively just as dead. It isn't real to me yet. They won't be in class tomorrow night, but I still won't believe it.'

'I know what you mean.'

'Let me know if anything happens, will you?'

'Of course.'

Anne Marie Stone lived in an apartment on the fifth floor of a walk-up on Grove Street in Greenwich Village, a block and a half from Sheridan Square. Levine found himself out of breath by the time he reached the third floor, and he stopped for a minute to get his wind back and to slow the pounding of his heart. There was no sound in the world quite as loud as the beating of his own heart these days, and when that beating grew too rapid or too irregular, Detective Levine felt a kind of panic that twenty-four years as a cop had never been able to produce.

He had to stop again at the fourth floor, and he remembered with envy what a Bostonian friend had told him about a city of Boston regulation that buildings used as residences had to have elevators if they were more than four stories high. Oh, to live in Boston. Or, even better, in Levittown, where there isn't a building higher than two stories anywhere.

He reached the fifth floor, finally, and knocked on the door of apartment 5B. Rustlings from within culminated in the peep-hole in the door being opened, and a blue eye peered suspiciously out at him. 'Who is it?' asked a muffled voice.

'Police,' said Levine. He dragged out his wallet, and held it high, so the eye in the peephole could read the identification.

'Second,' said the muffled voice, and the peephole closed. A seemingly endless series of rattles and clicks indicated locks being released, and then the door opened, and a short, slender girl, dressed in pink toreador pants, grey bulky sweater and blonde pony tail, motioned to Levine to come in. 'Have a seat,' she said, closing the door after him.

'Thank you.' Levine sat in a new-fangled basket chair, as uncomfortable as it looked, and the girl sat in another chair of the same type, facing him. But she managed to look comfortable in the thing.

'Is this something I did?' she asked him. 'Jaywalking or something?'

Levine smiled. No matter how innocent, a citizen always presumes himself guilty when the police come calling. 'No,' he said. 'It concerns two friends of yours, Al Gruber and Larry Perkins.'

'Those two?' The girl seemed calm, though curious, but not at all worried or apprehensive. She was still thinking in terms of something no more serious than jaywalking or a neighbour calling the police to complain about loud noises. 'What are they up to?'

'How close are you to them?'

The girl shrugged. 'I've gone out with both of them, that's all. We all take courses at Columbia. They're both nice guys, but there's nothing serious, you know. Not with either of them.'

'I don't know how to say this,' said Levine, 'except the blunt way. Early this afternoon, Perkins turned himself in and admitted he'd just killed Gruber.'

The girl stared at him. Twice, she opened her mouth to speak, but both times she closed it again. The silence lengthened, and Levine wondered belatedly if the girl had been telling the truth, if perhaps there had been something serious in her relationship with one of the boys after all. Then she blinked and looked away from him, clearing her throat. She stared out the window for a second, then looked back and said, 'He's pulling your leg.'

Levine shook his head. 'I'm afraid not.'

'Larry's got a weird sense of humour sometimes,' she said. 'It's a sick joke, that's all. Al's still around. You haven't found the body, have you?'

'I'm afraid we have. He was poisoned, and Perkins admitted he was the one who gave him the poison.'

'That little bottle Al had around the place? That was only a gag.'

'Not any more.'

She thought about it a minute longer, then shrugged, as though giving up the struggle to either believe or disbelieve. 'Why come to me?' she asked him.

'I'm not sure, to tell you the truth. Something smells wrong about the case, and I don't know what. There isn't any logic to it. I can't get through to Perkins, and it's too late to get through to Gruber. But I've got to get to know them both, if I'm going to understand what happened.'

'And you want me to tell you about them.'

'Yes.'

'Where did you hear about me? From Larry?'

'No, he didn't mention you at all. The gentlemanly instinct, I suppose. I talked to your teacher, Professor Stonegell.'

'I see.' She got up suddenly, in a single rapid and graceless movement, as though she had to make some motion, no matter how meaningless. 'Do you want some coffee?'

'Thank you, yes?'

'Come on along. We can talk while I get it ready.'

He followed her through the apartment. A hallway led from the long, narrow living room past bedroom and bathroom to a tiny kitchen. Levine sat down at the kitchen table, and Anne Marie Stone went through the motions of making coffee. As she worked, she talked.

'They're good friends,' she said. 'I mean, they *were* good friends. You know what I mean. Anyway, they're a lot different from each other. Oh, golly! I'm getting all loused up in tenses.'

'Talk as though both were alive,' said Levine. 'It should be easier that way.'

'I don't really believe it anyway,' she said. 'Al – he's a lot quieter than Larry. Kind of intense, you know? He's got a kind of reversed Messiah complex. You know, he figures he's supposed to be something great, a great writer, but he's afraid he doesn't have the stuff for it. So he worries about himself, and keeps trying to analyse himself, and he hates everything he writes because he doesn't think it's good enough for what he's supposed to be doing. That bottle of poison, that was a gag, you know, just a gag, but it was the kind of joke that has some sort of truth behind it. With this thing driving him like this, I suppose even death begins to look like a good escape after a while.'

She stopped her preparations with the coffee, and stood listening to what she had just said. 'Now he did escape, didn't he? I wonder if he'd thank Larry for taking the decision out of his hands.'

'Do you suppose he asked Larry to take the decision out of his hands?'

She shook her head. 'No. In the first place, Al could never ask anyone else to help him fight the thing out in any way. I know, I tried to talk to him a couple of times, but he just couldn't listen. It wasn't that he didn't want to listen, he just couldn't. He had to figure it out for himself. And Larry isn't the helpful sort, so Larry would be the last person anybody would go to for help. Not that Larry's a bad guy, really. He's just awfully self-centred. They both are, but in different ways. Al's always worried about himself, but Larry's always proud of himself. You know, Larry would say, "I'm for me first," and Al would say, "Am I worthy?" Something like that.'

'Had the two of them had a quarrel or anything recently, anything that you know of that might have prompted Larry to murder?'

'Not that I know of. They've both been getting more and more depressed, but neither of them blamed the other. Al blamed himself for not getting anywhere, and Larry blamed the stupidity of the world. You know, Larry wanted the same thing Al did, but Larry didn't worry about whether he was worthy or capable or anything like that. He once told me he wanted to be a famous writer, and he'd be one if he had to rob banks and use the money to bribe every publisher and editor and critic in the business. That was a gag, too, like Al's bottle of poison, but I think that one had some truth behind it, too.'

The coffee was ready, and she poured two cups, then sat down across from him. Levine added a bit of evaporated milk, but no sugar and stirred the coffee distractedly. 'I want to know why,' he said. 'Does that seem strange? Cops are supposed to want to know who, not why. I know who, but I want to know why.'

'Larry's the only one who could tell you, and I don't think he will.'

Levine drank some of the coffee, then got to his feet. 'Mind if I use your phone?' he asked.

'Go right ahead. It's in the living room, next to the bookcase.'

Levine walked back into the living room and called

the station. He asked for Crawley. When his partner came on the line, Levine said, 'Has Perkins signed the confession yet?'

'He's on the way down now. It's just been typed up.'

'Hold him there after he signs it, okay? I want to talk to him. I'm in Manhattan, starting back now.'

'What have you got?'

'I'm not sure I have anything. I just want to talk to Perkins again that's all.'

'Why sweat it? We got the body; we got the confession; we got the killer in a cell. Why make work for yourself?'

'I don't know. Maybe I'm just bored.'

'Okay, I'll hold him. Same room as before.'

Levine went back into the kitchen. 'Thank you for the coffee,' he said, 'If there's nothing else you can think of, I'll be leaving now.'

'Nothing,' she said. 'Larry's the only one can tell you why.'

She walked him to the front door, and he thanked her again as he was leaving. The stairs were a lot easier going down.

When Levine got back to the station, he picked up another plainclothesman, a detective named Ricco, a tall, athletic man in his middle thirties who affected the Ivy League look. He resembled more closely someone from the District Attorney's office than a precinct cop. Levine gave him a part to play, and the two of them went down the hall to the room where Perkins was waiting with Crawley.

'Perkins,' said Levine, the minute he walked in the room, before Crawley had a chance to give the game away by saying something to Ricco, 'This is Dan Ricco, a reporter from the *Daily News*.'

Perkins looked at Ricco with obvious interest, the first real display of interest and animation Levine had yet seen from him. 'A reporter?'

'That's right,' said Ricco. He looked at Levine. 'What is this?' He was playing it straight and blank.

'College student,' said Levine. 'Name's Larry Perkins.' He spelled the last name. 'He poisoned a fellow student.'

'Oh, yeah?' Ricco glanced at Perkins without much eagerness. 'What for?' he asked, looking back at Levine. 'Girl? Any sex in it?'

'Afraid not. It was some kind of intellectual motivation. They both wanted to be writers.'

Ricco shrugged. 'Two guys with the same job? What's so hot about that?'

'Well, the main thing,' said Levine, 'is that Perkins here wants to be famous. He tried to get famous by being a writer, but that wasn't working out. So he decided to be a famous murderer.'

Ricco looked at Perkins. 'Is that right?' he asked.

Perkins was glowering at them all, but especially at Levine. 'What difference does it make?' he said.

'The kid's going to get the chair, of course,' said Levine blandly. 'We have his signed confession and everything. But I've kind of taken a liking to him. I'd hate to see him throw his life away without getting something for it. I thought maybe you could get him a nice headline on page two, something he could hang up on the wall of his cell.'

Ricco chuckled and shook his head. 'Not a chance of it,' he said. 'Even if I wrote the story big, the city desk would knock it down to nothing. This kind of story is a dime a dozen. People kill other people around New York twenty-four hours a day. Unless there's a good strong sex interest, or it's maybe one of those mass killings things like the guy who put the bomb in the airplane, a murder in New York is filler stuff. And who needs filler stuff in the spring, when the ball teams are just getting started?'

'You've got influence on the paper, Dan,' said Levine. 'Couldn't you at least get him picked up by the wire services?'

'Not a chance in a million. What's he done that a few hundred other clucks in New York don't do every year? Sorry, Abe, I'd like to do you the favour, but it's no go.'

Levine sighed. 'Okay, Dan,' he said. 'If you say so.'

'Sorry,' said Ricco. He grinned at Perkins. 'Sorry, kid,' he said, 'You should of knifed a chorus girl or something.'

Ricco left and Levine glanced at Crawley, who was

industriously yanking on his ear-lobe and looking bewildered. Levine sat down facing Perkins and said, 'Well?'

'Let me alone a minute,' snarled Perkins. 'I'm trying to think.'

'I was right, wasn't I?' asked Levine. 'You wanted to go out in a blaze of glory.'

'All right, all right. Al took his way, I took mine. What's the difference?'

'No difference,' said Levine. He got wearily to his feet, and headed for the door. 'I'll have you sent back to your cell now.'

'Listen,' said Perkins suddenly. 'You know I didn't kill him, don't you? You know he committed suicide, don't you?'

Levine opened the door and motioned to the two uniformed cops waiting in the hall.

'Wait,' said Perkins desperately.

'I know, I know,' said Levine, 'Gruber really killed himself, and I suppose you burned the note he left.'

'You know damn well I did.'

'That's too bad, boy.'

Perkins didn't want to leave. Levine watched deadpan as the boy was led away, and then he allowed himself to relax, let the tension drain out of him. He sagged into a chair and studied the veins on the backs of his hands.

Crawley said, into the silence, 'What was all that about, Abe?'

'Just what you heard.'

'Gruber committed suicide?'

'They both did.'

'Well – what are we going to do now?'

'Nothing. We investigated; we got a confession; we made an arrest. Now we're done.'

'But –'

'But hell!' Levine glared at his partner. 'That little fool is gonna go to trial, Jack, and he's gonna be convicted and go to the chair. He chose it himself. It was *his* choice. I'm not railroading him; he chose his own end. And he's going to get what he wanted.'

'But listen, Abe –'

'I won't listen!'

'Let me – let me get a word in.'

Levine was on his feet suddenly, and now it all came boiling out, the indignation and the rage and the frustration. 'Damn it, you don't know yet! You've got another six, seven years yet. You don't know what it feels like to lie awake in bed at night and listen to your heart skip a beat every once in a while, and wonder when it's going to skip two beats in a row and you're dead. You don't know what it feels like to know your body's starting to die, it's starting to get old and die and it's all downhill from now on.'

'What's that got to do with –'

'I'll tell you what! They had the *choice*! Both of them young, both of them with sound bodies and sound hearts and years ahead of them, decades ahead of them. And they chose to throw it away! They chose to throw away what I don't have any more. Don't you think I wish *I* had that choice? All right! They chose to die, let 'em die!'

Levine was panting from exertion, leaning over the desk and shouting in Jack Crawley's face. And now, in the sudden silence while he wasn't speaking, he heard the ragged rustle of his breath, felt the tremblings of nerve and muscle throughout his body. He let himself carefully down into a chair and sat there, staring at the wall, trying to get his breath.

Jack Crawley was saying something, far away, but Levine couldn't hear him. He was listening to something else, the loudest sound in all the world. The fitful throbbing of his own heart.

The Mystery of the Raymond Mortgage

F. Scott Fitzgerald

When I first saw John Syrel of the New York *Daily News*, he was standing before an open window of my house gazing out on the city. It was about six o'clock and the lights were just going on. All down Thirty-third Street was a long line of gaily illuminated buildings. He was not a tall man, but thanks to the erectness of his posture and the suppleness of his movement, it would take no athlete to tell that he was of fine build. He was twenty-three years old when I first saw him, and was already a reporter on the *News*. He was not a handsome man; his face was clean-shaven, and his chin showed him to be of strong character. His eyes and hair were brown.

As I entered the room he turned around slowly and addressed me in a slow, drawling tone: 'I think I have the honour of speaking to Mr Egan, Chief of Police.' I assented, and he went on: 'My name is John Syrel and my business, to tell you frankly, is to learn all I can about the case of the Raymond mortgage.'

I started to speak but he silenced me with a wave of his hand. 'Though I belong to the staff of the *Daily News*,' he continued, 'I am not here as an agent of the paper.'

'I am not here,' I interrupted coldly, 'to tell every newspaper reporter or adventurer about private affairs. James, show this man out.'

Syrel turned without a word and I heard his steps echo up the driveway.

However, this was not destined to be the last time I ever saw Syrel, as events will show.

The morning after I first saw John Syrel, I proceeded to the scene of the crime to which he had alluded. On the train I picked up a newspaper and read the following account of the crime and theft:

EXTRA

Great Crime Committed in
Suburbs of City
Mayor Proceeding to Scene
of Crime

> On the morning of July 1st a crime and serious theft were committed on the outskirts of the city. Miss Raymond was killed and the body of a servant was found outside of the house. Mr Raymond of Santuka Lake was awakened on Tuesday morning by a scream and two revolver shots which proceeded from his wife's room. He tried to open the door but it would not open. He was almost certain the door was locked from the inside, when suddenly it swung open disclosing a room in frightful disorder. On the centre of the floor was a revolver and on his wife's bed was a bloodstain in the shape of a hand. His wife was missing, but on a closer search he found his daughter under the bed, stone dead. The window was broken in two places. Miss Raymond had a bullet wound on her body and her head was fearfully cut. The body of a servant was found outside with a bullet hole through his head. Mrs Raymond has not been found.
>
> The room was upset. The bureau drawers were out as if the murderer had been looking for something. Chief of Police Egan is on the scene of the crime, etc.

Just then the conductor called out 'Santuka!' The train came to a stop, and getting out of the car I walked up to the house. On the porch I met Gregson, who was supposed to be the ablest detective in the force. He gave me a plan of the house which he said he would like to have me look at before we went in.

'The body of the servant,' he said, 'is that of John Standish. He has been with the family twelve years and was a perfectly honest man. He was only thirty-two years old.'

'The bullet which killed him was not found?' I asked.

'No,' he answered, and then, 'Well, you had better come and see for yourself. By the way, there was a fellow hanging around here who was trying to see the body. When I refused to let him in, he went around to where the servant was shot and I saw him go down on his knees on the grass and begin to search. A few minutes later he stood up and leaned against a tree. Then he came up to the house and asked to see the body again. I said he could if he would go away afterwards. He assented, and when he got inside the room he went down on his knees under the bed and hunted around. Then he went over to the window and examined the broken pane carefully. After that he declared himself satisfied and went down towards the hotel.'

After I had examined the room to my satisfaction, I found that I might as well try to see through a millstone as to try to fathom this mystery. As I finished my investigation I met Gregson in the laboratory.

'I suppose you heard about the mortgage,' said he, as we went down stairs. I answered in the negative, and he told me that a valuable mortgage had disappeared from the room in which Miss Raymond was killed. The night before, Mr Raymond had placed the mortgage in a drawer and it had disappeared.

On my way to town that night I met Syrel again, and he bowed cordially to me. I began to feel ashamed of myself for sending him out of my house. As I went into the car the only vacant seat was next to him. I sat down and apologized for my rudeness of the day before. He took it lightly and, there being nothing to say, we sat in silence. At last I ventured a remark.

'What do you think of the case?'

'I don't think anything of it as yet. I haven't had time yet.'

Nothing daunted, I began again. 'Did you learn anything?'

Syrel dug his hand into his pocket and produced a bullet. I examined it.

'Where did you find it?' I asked.

'In the yard,' he answered briefly.

At this I again relapsed into my seat. When we reached the city, night was coming on. My first day's investigation was not very successful.

My next day's investigation was no more successful than the first. My friend Syrel was not at home. The maid came into Mr Raymond's room while I was there and gave notice that she was going to leave. 'Mr Raymond,' she said, 'there was queer noises outside my window last night. I'd like to stay, sir, but it grates on my nerves.'

Beyond this nothing happened, and I came home worn out.

On the morning of the next day I was awakened by the maid who had a telegram in her hand. I opened it and found it was from Gregson. 'Come at once,' it said, 'startling development.'

I dressed hurriedly and took the first car to Santuka. When I reached the Santuka station, Gregson was waiting for me in a runabout. As soon as I got into the carriage Gregson told me what had happened.

'Someone was in the house last night. You know Mr Raymond asked me to sleep there. Well, last night, about one, I began to be very thirsty. I went into the hall to get a drink from the faucet there, and as I was passing from my room (I sleep in Miss Raymond's room) into the hall I heard somebody in Mrs Raymond's room. Wondering why Mr Raymond was up at that time of night I went into the sitting-room to investigate. I opened the door to Mrs Raymond's room. The body of Miss Raymond was lying on the sofa. A man was kneeling beside it. His face was away from me, but I could tell by his figure that he was not Mr Raymond. As I looked he got up softly and I saw him open a bureau drawer. He took something out and put it into his pocket. As he turned around he saw me, and I saw that he was a young man. With a cry of rage he sprang at me, and having no weapon I retreated. He snatched up a heavy Indian club and swung it over my head. I gave a cry which must have alarmed the house, for I knew nothing more till I saw Mr Raymond bending over me.'

‘How did this man look?’ I asked. ‘Would you know him if you saw him again?’

‘I think not,’ he answered. ‘I only saw his profile.’

‘The only explanation I can give is this,’ said I. ‘The murderer was in Miss Raymond’s room and when she came in he overpowered her and inflicted the gash. He then made for Mrs Raymond’s room and carried her off after having first shot Miss Raymond, who attempted to rise. Outside the house he met Standish, who attempted to stop him and was shot.’

Gregson smiled. ‘That solution is impossible,’ he said.

As we reached the house I saw John Syrel, who beckoned me aside. ‘If you come with me,’ he said, ‘you will learn something that may be valuable to you.’

I excused myself to Gregson and followed Syrel. As we reached the walk he began to talk.

‘Let us suppose that the murderer or murderess escaped from the house. Where would they go? Naturally they wanted to get away. Where did they go? Now, there are two railroad stations near by, Santuka and Lidgeville. I have ascertained that they did not go by Santuka. So did Gregson. I supposed, therefore, that they went by Lidgeville. Gregson didn’t. That’s the difference. A straight line between here and Lidgeville. At first there was nothing. About two miles farther on I saw some footprints in a marshy hollow. They consisted of three footprints. I took an impression. Here it is. You see this one is a woman’s. I have compared it with one of Mrs Raymond’s boots. They are identical. The others are mates. They belong to a man.

‘I compared the bullet I found, where Standish was killed, with one of the remaining cartridges in the revolver that was found in Mrs Raymond’s room. They were mates. Only one shot had been fired and as I had found one bullet, I concluded that either Mrs or Miss Raymond had fired the shot. I preferred to think Mrs Raymond fired it because she had fled.

‘Summing these up and also taking into consideration that Mrs Raymond must have had some cause to try to kill Standish, I concluded that John Standish killed Miss Raymond through the window of her mother’s room, Friday night. I also conclude that Mrs Raymond after ascertaining that her daughter was dead shot Standish through the window and killed him. Horrified at what she had done she hid behind the door when Mr Raymond came in. Then she ran down the back stairs. Going outside she stumbled upon the revolver Standish had used and picking it up took it with her. Somewhere between here and Lidgeville she met the owner of these footprints either by accident or design and walked with him to the station where they took the early train for Chicago. The stationmaster did not see the man. He says that only a woman bought a ticket, so I concluded that the young man didn't go. Now you must tell me what Gregson told you.'

'How did you know all this,' I exclaimed, astonished. And then I told him about the midnight visitor. He did not appear to be much astonished, and he said, 'I guess that the young man is our friend of the footprints. Now you had better get a brace of revolvers and pack your suitcase if you wish to go with me to find this young man and Mrs Raymond, who I think is with him.'

Greatly surprised at what I had heard, I took the first train back to town. I bought a pair of fine Colt revolvers, a dark lantern, and two changes of clothing. We went over to Lidgeville and found that a young man had left on the six o'clock train for Ithaca.

On reaching Ithaca we found that he had changed trains and was now halfway to Princeton, New Jersey. It was five o'clock but we took a fast train and expected to overtake him halfway between Ithaca and Princeton. What was our chagrin when on reaching the slow train, to find he had gotten off at Indianous and was now probably safe.

Thoroughly disappointed, we took the train for Indianous. The ticket seller said that a young man in a light grey suit had taken a bus to the Raswell Hotel. We found the bus which the stationmaster said he had taken, in the street. We went up to the driver and he admitted that he had started for the Raswell Hotel in his cab.

'But,' said the old fellow, 'when I reached there, the fellow had clean disappeared, an' I never got his fare.'

Syrel groaned; it was plain that we had lost the young

man. We took the next train for New York and telegraphed to Mr Raymond that we would be down Monday. Sunday night, however, I was called to the phone and recognized Syrel's voice. He directed me to come at once to 534 Chestnut Street. I met him on the doorstep.

'What have you heard?' I asked.

'I have an agent in Indianous,' he replied, 'in the shape of an Arab boy whom I employ for ten cents a day. I told him to spot the woman and today I got a telegram from him (I left him money to send one) saying to come at once. So come on.'

We took the train for Indianous. 'Smidy,' the young Arab, met us at the station.

'You see, sir, it's dis way. You says, "Spot de guy wid dat hack," and I says I would. Dat night a young dude comes out of de house on Pine Street and gives the cabman a ten-dollar bill. An' den he went back into the house and a minute after he comes out wid a woman, an' den day went down here a little way an' goes into a house farther down the street.'

We followed Smidy down the street until we arrived at a corner house. The ground floor was occupied by a cigar store, but the second floor was evidently for rent. As we stood there a face appeared at the window and, seeing us, hastily retreated.

Syrel pulled a picture from his pocket. 'It's she,' he exclaimed, and calling us to follow he dashed into a little side door. We heard voices upstairs, a shuffle of feet and a noise as if a door had been shut.

'Up the stairs,' shouted Syrel, and we followed him, taking two steps at a bound. As we reached the top landing we were met by a young man.

'What right have you to enter this house?' he demanded.

'The right of the law,' replied Syrel.

'I didn't do it,' broke out the young man. 'It was this way. Agnes Raymond loved me—she did not love Standish—he shot her; and God did not let her murder go unrevenged. It was well Mrs Raymond killed him, for his blood would have been on my hands. I went back to see Agnes before she was buried. A man came in. I knocked him down. I didn't know until a moment ago that Mrs Raymond had killed him.'

'I forgot Mrs Raymond,' screamed Syrel. 'Where is she?'

'She is out of your power forever,' said the young man.

Syrel brushed past him and, with Smidy and me following, burst open the door of the room at the head of the stairs. We rushed in.

On the floor lay a woman, and as soon as I touched her heart I knew she was beyond the doctor's skill.

'She has taken poison,' I said.

Syrel looked around—the young man had gone. And we stood there aghast in the presence of death.

Points for Discussion and Writing

THE GATEWOOD CAPER

Points for discussion

1 What does the opening sentence suggest about the position held by Harvey Gatewood—or about his organization?
2 What does his attitude to the detective suggest about his view of himself? What does the detective say that confirms this?
3 What do we learn about the detective from his first conversation with Gatewood? What does the question of the payment of the ransom tell us about Gatewood? – the detective?
4 What do we learn of the relationship between Gatewood and his daughter?
5 What does the London tailor's label, the bushel of photographs, the great stack of letters tell us about the girl?
6 Is Gatewood consistent in his attitudes – to the note – the phone call? How does he react under stress?
7 How does Hammett build up the tension in the payment scene?
8 Why is it partially Gatewood's own fault if they cannot identify the woman? Is it to be expected that he will blame others?
9 What do we learn about Gatewood and the detective in the hours after the ransom has been paid?
10 What is implied by '. . . the worst that could be said about Audrey was that she was her father's own daughter'? How has she justified this remark?

Writing possibilities

1 Look closely at the description of Gatewood and note how much of appearance and character are conveyed by pictorial language. Write a similar description of a similar English type.

2 Notice Hammett's method of building tension – the payment scene, the recognition of 'Penny' Quayle. Use the method to build a tense scene of your own.
3 'Her father's own daughter.' Write a story in which the characteristics shared by father and daughter, or mother and son, cause a clash between them.
4 Justice triumphs in the end. Who wins? Where do your sympathies lie? Has there been any attempt to enlist your sympathies for any of the characters. Write a short piece giving your views of the people involved in *The Gatewood Caper.*

TO HAVE AND HAVE NOT

Points for discussion

1 What does Harry's reaction – or lack of reaction – to the bank robbery suggest to you about him? How does the author emphasise this?
2 What is the effect of the death of Albert upon the reader? What does it show about the men Harry is to deal with?
3 Select those details from the story that indicate that Harry knew his business as a charter-boat captain.
4 At what moment in the story does Harry decide that he must act to save his own life and revenge the death of Albert?
5 What makes Roberto the most dangerous of the Cubans? How do the others feel about him?
6 When Harry goes to check the engines he thinks about Albert. Does he think as little about throwing him overboard as his words make out?
7 What purpose of the author is served by the conversation Harry has with the boy.
8 Why did the drink that Harry took have no effect on the 'dank cold part that had spread from his stomach to all over the inside of his chest'? What does warm it?
9 How does Harry function when the action starts? After he has been hit?
10 What are your reactions to this story of violent action? Do you feel that the motives of the Cubans or Harry justified what they did?

Writing possibilities

1 The boy seems to think that the revolution justifies everything; Harry is far from sure. Write two paragraphs, each arguing one point of view. Then write a paragraph giving your conclusions.
2 Tell part of the story as Harry might have told it after some years had passed.

3. Hemingway considered the most difficult part of writing was putting down 'what really happened in action'. Try to write an action sequence as objectively and accurately as he does. If you like, rewrite the action sequence in this story in your own words.
4. *To Have and Have Not* (the full novel) became the basis of a screenplay. It departed considerably from the original. Can you suggest how you would film the sequence you have read?

I'LL BE WAITING

Points for discussion

1. Does Tony Reseck look like your image of a detective? What qualities does he possess that suggest he might be a very efficient one?
2. What is Tony afraid the girl might be preparing to do? What leads him to this belief?
3. What type of atmosphere does the author create in this story? What are the details he uses to achieve this?
4. What does the porter fear is going to happen to Tony?
5. How does Tony feel about his brother Al? What does he say that shows his feelings? How does Al feel?
6. What is Tony's relationship with the other members of the hotel staff? Why should he be so disturbed at not being informed of the letting of another room?
7. What do we learn about Tony Reseck from his conversation with the man in 14B? Who is he thinking of when he says: 'Mugs. Guys with guns. Just mugs.'?
8. What is implied in 'They'll send you violets'?
9. What is in Tony's mind when he says: 'Nobody's all bad'?
10. How had Al out-thought his brother? With what result? What does Tony's reaction to the news tell us?

Writing possibilities

1. 'Still the funny little fat guy, eh, Tony?', 'You're a good brother, Tony', 'Hurry back, pop', 'You're a funny little guy', 'You're a sweet little guy, Tony', 'You're the boss'. Give your opinion of Tony Resek from the facts as you know them.
2. In the section where Tony visits 14B the author builds up the tension with short sentences and detached phrases. Examine this section and then try a similar piece of writing.
3. In other sections of the story he creates an atmosphere of calm and waiting. Find these sections, try to discover how the effect is created and see if you can do the same.

4 'Sure. Not a thing for me to do. Don't know why they pay me.' Describe the events of Tony's evening from the point of view of the girl, the desk-clerk, Al.

THE SNATCHING OF BOOKIE BOB

Points for discussion

1 What sort of living conditions does the narrator regard as heart-touching? Do you agree?

2 What is ironic about the moral indignation of the Manhattan citizens on the subject of 'snatching'? Can you find other similar examples of irony?

3 What are the essentials of a well-prepared and well-executed act of 'snatching'?

4 In what ways does 'snatching' differ from kidnapping? Why do you think the author makes these distinctions?

5 What do we learn of the narrator – his habits, his haunts, his relationships with the crooks, his attitude towards women?

6 What is strange about the standards of conduct and honour among the crooks? What are their ideas of right and wrong?

7 What evidence does the narrator give or imply to prove that Bookie Bob is mean?

8 What methods of 'persuasion' does Harry the Horse appear to prefer?

9 What would appear to be the relationship between Bookie Bob and the crooks? Is this in keeping with the rest of the story?

10 What does the last line indicate about Bookie Bob's 'knowledge' of his wife? Who gets the greatest benefit from the snatching of Bookie Bob?

Writing possibilities

1 'Runyonese', as the slang Damon Runyon used to tell his stories is called, contains a great many terms unusual to our ears. Nearly all of them are obvious from their context. In case any of your classmates have difficulty, make them a glossary, e.g. scratch – money; mobbed up with – part of a gang containing.

2 Try to write a story about English crooks using today's slang.

3 Spend a little time with Eric Partridge's *Dictionary of Slang and Unconventional English* and *Dictionary of the Underworld*, and write a short piece about the peculiarities of language.

4 Damon Runyon's style relies upon unfailing use of the present tense. Examine several paragraphs and then try this form of writing yourself.

THE DAY OF THE BULLET

Points for discussion

1 What do you understand by the phrase 'a day of destiny'? Do you believe in such a day?
2 Why does the author stress the peace and serenity of the neighbourhood in which the two boys grew up?
3 What do you learn of Mr Rose from his attitude and actions with the two boys? Is this confirmed in any way later in the story?
4 Why did Iggy hero-worship his father? What importance has this for the story?
5 Why is it necessary to the story that the golf course should be of the type that was often empty?
6 '*This* is who I am!' Who or what is Mr Rose? What has the small man done?
7 Which of the two boys' attitudes do you consider the most sensible? Did the small man want their help? Why did he react in the way he did?
8 The narrator thinks that Iggy wants to get his own back on Mr Rose. Mr Rose suggests as much himself. Do you think this is Iggy's real reason?
9 Why, do you think, do the sergeant of police and Iggy's father treat Iggy in the way that they do?
10 What makes Iggy talk of his father and Mr Rose in the way he does, and how does it link up with the opening of the story?

Writing possibilities

1 This is a story of disillusionment – a story in which a boy learns that right does not always triumph, that justice is not always done. Can you write a similar story based upon your own experience.
2 The narrator and Iggy see something that they were not intended to see, and their subsequent actions get them into trouble. Use this as the basis for a story of your own.
3 Iggy was 'golf-crazy'. Can you understand why anyone should be so obsessed with a sport or hobby? Do you feel this way about anything? Why?
4 Can you look back on a day of destiny in your life? If so, describe it, and say what difference it made to you.

THE LIAR

Points for discussion

1 In what part of America does this story take place? What evidence have you for your opinion?

2 What is the attitude of the newcomer to those already there?

3 '. . . the humour he achieved and which they understood.' How is Ek's humour achieved?

4 What is the attitude of the others towards the story-teller? How does he react to this?

5 Who would appear to be the natural leader of the group? What evidence have you for this?

6 What type of people would you expect to find living in the type of country that Ek describes?

7 How did Ek know he wasn't far from the man who had killed the rattlers? Why do you think the author stresses this?

8 What is the woman trying to do when she flings herself upon the neck of the second man? What do you suppose she would be saying?

9 Is there any significance in the effect of the stranger's gaze upon Ek? What thought begins to form in your mind at this point in the story?

10 What is ironic in 'knowing his veracity as a liar was gone forever'? What is the importance of using Gibson to deliver the parting shot?

Writing possibilities

1 Ek describes the incidents at the farm from a distant viewpoint. His account of what happened is deduction rather than knowledge – he knows none of the participants and hears nothing that is said. Can you write an account which contains the same incidents but has another explanation?

2 Write a similar account from a distant viewpoint so that the motives of the participants are made clear through their actions.

3 Ek specializes in telling 'stretchers', tall tales, big windies – a form of artistic lying using exaggeration to create humour. Study Ek's method in the story of the Mitchell family, and his introduction to shoes, and then create a 'whopper' of your own.

4 '. . . a long saturnine face in which his two bleached eyes were innocent and keen – like a depraved priest . . .', 'they was clamped together like two sheep in a storm', 'the hot black gaze of the stranger seemed like a blade spitting him against the wall, like a pinned moth'. Attempt some similes of your own to convey character or action.

IT TAKES A THIEF

Points for discussion

1 What do you understand by the phrase 'a nice family and a nice home'? Collect details from the text to support your view.
2 Why do you think Mr Shelton 'did fine. Very, very fine'? What explanation does the author give later on?
3 Why do you think the safe was situated in the place it was?
4 Why was Mrs Shelton disturbed over the 'phone call that Shelton was making? What idea made them 'too frightened to speak for a few minutes'?
5 What is ironic in Shelton's words: 'They never catch thieves.'?
6 How does the author stress Shelton's obsession with the money and what it means to him?
7 Why, do you think, did the detective not produce the money at first? Is the detective suspicious of Shelton? What evidence have you for your opinion?
8 What sign was Shelton looking for in the detective's eyes – searching for in his expression?
9 What will the detectives 'start looking around' for? For what are the Sheltons waiting?
10 What is the significance of the title of the story?

Writing possibilities

1 This story illustrates a well-known proverb. Write a story based upon a similar proverb: Too many cooks . . . , A bird in the hand . . . , Sauce for the goose . . . , etc.
2 Write about a situation in which you lose something at home or in school and dare not claim it back.
3 In the opening paragraphs of this story much is implied but little is actually stated openly. Write a similar series of paragraphs implying much more than you actually say.
4 'He simply stood there, the law with two little black eyes.' Can you write some equally succinct potted pictures?

GOODBYE, POPS

Points for discussion

1 What is the first indication of suspense in the story? When do you get an explanation for the narrator's tension?
2 What do we learn of the narrator's character from his reaction to the hackie's attitude? Suggest other exchanges with other characters that confirm this.

3 What do we learn of the character of the narrator from his approach to the house? Give other evidence from the text which agrees with this.
4 What is the emotional relationship between the narrator and other members of his family apart from Pops? Can you suggest why this should be so?
5 What does the encounter with the Doctor tell you about the narrator's attitude to his father?
6 What is the significance of the images of the foxhound and bobcat, and the weasel in a trap?
7 What did Chris and his father have to share? Collect evidence for your answer from the text.
8 Is there any more to Rod's words – 'You – you murderous animal' – than the obvious insult?
9 In your opinion how responsible was Chris for the death of the old farmer in the car.
10 'I felt like a marten in a brooding house.' Explain. With whom do your sympathies lie in this story? Try to explain why. Has the author made the 'good' people unsympathetic? How?
11 What is the point of Chris's tribute to his father? Why does it take the form it does?
12 Do you find the ending of the story satisfactory? – too predictable? – in keeping with the imagery of the hunt?

Writing possibilities

1 This is a story of family tensions caused by the differing attitudes to life of the members of the family. Write a story with a similar theme.
2 Chris enjoys hunting and shooting. What is your attitude towards such sports and why?
3 The author uses similes closely connected with Chris's main interest. Can you write a character sketch using imagery in a similar way?
4 Chris is a mixture of good and evil – great love for his father and hatred and contempt for others. Write two paragraphs: one in his defence, the other attacking him. Write a third paragraph containing your own conclusions about him.

THE BEST FRIEND MURDER

Points for discussion

1 What characteristics of Abe Levine does the author stress in the early paragraphs? How important is this in understanding the climax of the story.
2 Why is Abe so concerned about methods of murder?

3 Reread the section where the detectives enter the room containing the body. Does anything strike you about the order in which the items are described?
4 Why is Crawley interested in Al Gruber's typewriter? What might have been written there?
5 Gather textual evidence of those things that make Abe Levine feel uneasy about Perkins and the situation.
6 Abe detects pleading in Perkins' eyes. What do you think Perkins was pleading for – acceptance of his story or exoneration from guilt?
7 What characteristics of (a) Al Gruber, (b) Perkins are emphasized by the Superintendent, the Professor, and his girl friend? How far is this confirmed by Gruber's notebook?
8 What is the significance of the shouts of 'Al! Al!' that the Superintendent heard?
9 How does the author reintroduce Abe Levine's concern with his heart?
10 What does Levine believe about Perkins that leads him to introduce Ricco as a reporter?

Writing possibilities

1 There are a number of two or three line descriptions of characters in the story. They convey a great deal in few words. Try writing similar short descriptions of real or imaginary people.
2 Levine's method of getting to know a suspect was to fit him into a type and then look for small and individual ways in which he differed from the general type. Allocate your friends and acquaintances to their stereotypes and then indicate those things that give them their individuality.
3 Write a description of a room with the same economy used in the description of Gruber's apartment.
4 The point of the story is the attitude taken by Abe Levine because of his age and state of health. Can you work out a story based upon the reaction of a character suffering from some disability – partial paralysis, short-sightedness, a lost limb, deafness – to another character who does not appreciate his health advantage.

THE MYSTERY OF THE RAYMOND MORTGAGE

Points for discussion

1 What do we learn of Mr Egan from the first exchange with John Syrel?
2 What do we learn of John Syrel?

3 What is unusual, according to today's procedures, about the methods of travel adopted by the Chief of Police?
4 What details do you find lacking in the newspaper report?
5 Who do you think was the man conducting his own investigation? Is this plausible?
6 What does the second meeting of Egan and Syrel show us about both men?
7 Why is Gregson so sure that Mr Egan's solution to the mystery is impossible?
8 Does Syrel's account of his investigations throw any doubt upon Egan's statement that Gregson is 'supposed to be the ablest detective in the force'?
9 What is meant in this context by 'young Arab'?
10 This story was written by a famous author when he was only 13 years old. Can you detect traces of the talent that was to make him 'the voice of his generation'?

Writing possibilities

1 This was written by a thirteen-year-old. Do you think there are any sections which could be improved? Re-write them.
2 Can you construct and write a similar mystery story with all the clues and twists in the plot that such a story involves.
3 This story obviously owes something to the stories about Sherlock Holmes and Watson. Read one or two of these and write a comparison.

Further Reading

'. . . once again, it would be wrong for the teacher to condemn the whole genre altogether; his job is to discriminate and select.'

Nicholas Tucker, *Understanding the Mass Media,* 1966.

1. This booklist is far from comprehensive. It includes relevant material from the authors included in the anthology, and some of the more readily available examples of the genre.

CHANDLER, Raymond

The Big Sleep, Hamish Hamilton, 1939; Penguin, 1948.
Farewell My Lovely, Hamish Hamilton, 1940; Penguin, 1949.
The High Window, Hamish Hamilton, 1943; Penguin, 1951.
The Lady in the Lake, Hamish Hamilton, 1944; Penguin, 1952.
The Little Sister, Hamish Hamilton, 1949; Penguin, 1955.

Short Stories

Trouble is My Business, Penguin, 1950.
Pearls are a Nuisance, Hamish Hamilton, 1950; Penguin, 1964.
Smart Aleck Kill, Hamish Hamilton, 1958; Penguin, 1964.

ELLIN, Stanley

Dreadful Summit, Boardman, 1958; Penguin, 1964.
The Valentine Estate, Macdonald, 1968; Penguin, 1972.

Short Stories

The Speciality of the House, Boardman, 1957; Penguin, 1968.
The Blessington Method, Michael Joseph, 1965; Penguin, 1971.

FAULKNER, William

Sanctuary, Chatto and Windus, 1966; Penguin, 1970.
The Essential Faulkner, Chatto and Windus, 1967.
Intruder in the Dust, Chatto and Windus, 1968; Penguin, 1970.
New Orleans Sketches, Chatto and Windus, 1968.

FITZGERALD, Francis Scott

The Great Gatsby, Penguin, 1969.
Diamond as Big as the Ritz and other stories, Penguin, 1969.

GORES, Joe

Mr Gores's short stories of Daniel Kearny Associates, a skiptracing agency, have so far appeared in *Ellery Queen's Mystery Magazine*, and anthologies.

HAMMETT, Dashiell

The Maltese Falcon, Cassell, 1930; Penguin, 1963.
The Dain Curse, Cassell, 1931; Penguin, 1966.
The Thin Man, Cassell, 1932; Penguin, 1935.
Red Harvest, Cassell, 1950; Penguin, 1963.

Short Stories

The Dashiell Hammett Story Omnibus, Cassell, 1966; Penguin (as *The Big Knockover and other stories*), 1970.

HEMINGWAY, Ernest

Men without Women, Jonathan Cape, 1928; Penguin, 1969.
To Have and Have Not, Jonathan Cape, 1937; Penguin, 1969.
First Forty-nine Stories, Jonathan Cape, 1939.

MILLER, Arthur

I don't Need You Any More and other stories, Penguin, 1969.

RUNYON, Damon

Runyon on Broadway, Constable, 1950.
Runyon from First to Last, Constable, 1954.

WESTLAKE, Donald E.

The Busy Body, Boardman, 1966; Penguin, 1967.
Killing Time, Boardman, 1962; Penguin, 1966.
The Mercenaries, Boardman, 1961; Four Square, 1963; Penguin, 1970.
The Hot Rock, Hodder, 1971.

SHAW, Joseph T., *The Hard-boiled Omnibus*, Simon and Schuster, 1946.
GOULART, Ron, *The Hardboiled Dicks*, Boardman, 1967.
BOUCHER, Anthony, *Great American Detective Stories*, World Publishing Company, 1945.
BOUCHER, Anthony, *Best American Detective Stories of the Year*, a series published by T. V. Boardman annually.
QUEEN, Ellery, *The Queen's Awards*; *Ellery Queen's Mystery Annuals*; *Ellery Queen's Anthologies*, series published between 1954 and 1969, mainly by Victor Gollancz.
COOKE, David C., *My Best Murder Story*, Boardman, 1957.
RICHARDSON, Maurice, *American Detective Stories*, Pilot Press, 1943.
BURNETT, W. R., *The Asphalt Jungle*, Macdonald, 1950; Corgi, 1955. *Little Caesar*, Jonathan Cape, 1929. *High Sierra*, Kaye and Ward, 1968.
FAIR, A. A., *Lam to the Slaughter* and many others featuring Donald Lam, a small but intelligent private eye. (A. A. Fair is a pseudonym of Erle Stanley Gardner.)
GARDNER, Erle Stanley, *The Case of the Screaming Woman* and many, many others featuring Perry Mason.
McBAIN, Ed, *Cop Hater* and many others featuring the detectives of the 87th Precinct. (Ed McBain is a pseudonym of Evan Hunter.)
MACDONALD, Ross, *The Moving Target* and others featuring Lew Archer, possible successor to Raymond Chandler's Philip Marlowe.
PIKE, Robert L., *Bullitt*, Andre Deutsch, 1965; Penguin, 1969.

2 Criticism

CHANDLER, Raymond, 'The Simple Art of Murder' in *The Smell of Fear*, Hamish Hamilton, 1944; or *Pearls are a Nuisance*, Penguin, 1969.
DURHAM, Philip, *Down These Mean Streets a Man Must Go*, Chapel Hill, 1963.
GILBERT, Michael (editor), *Crime in Good Company*, Constable, 1959.
GOULART, Ron, Introduction to *The Hardboiled Dicks*, Boardman, 1965.
HALL, Stuart & WHANNEL, Paddy, 'The Avenging Angels' in *The Popular Arts*, Hutchinson, 1964.
HAYCRAFT, Howard, *Murder for Pleasure* (1942).
HEATH, R. B., *Popular Reading*, The Bodley Head, 1968.
HOGGART, Richard, 'The Newer Mass Art: Sex and Violence Novels' in *The Uses of Literacy*, Chatto and Windus, 1957.

MAUGHAM, W. Somerset, 'The Decline and Fall of the Detective Story' in *The Vagrant Mood*, Heinemann, 1952.
MURCH, A. E., *The Development of the Detective Novel*, Peter Owen, 1958.
ROUTLEY, E., *The Puritan Pleasures of the Detective Story*, Gollancz, 1972.
SHAW, Joseph T., Introduction to *The Hard-Boiled Omnibus*, Simon and Schuster, 1946.
SIMISTER, O. E., 'Detective Stories' in *The School Librarian*, Vol. 8, No. 6, 1957.
SCOTT, Sutherland, *Blood in Their Ink*, Stanley Paul, 1953.
SYMONS, Julian, *Bloody Murder*, Faber and Faber, 1972. 'Marlowe's Victim (Raymond Chandler)' in *Critical Occasions*, Hamish Hamilton, 1962.
TUCKER, Nicholas, Reference pp. 161–163 in *Understanding the Mass Media*, Cambridge University Press, 1966.
WATSON, Colin, *Snobbery with Violence*, Eyre and Spottiswoode, 1971.
WOOD, Michael, 'The Cost of Money' (Ross Macdonald) in *New Society*, 30th December 1971.

Films

'The film (The Maltese Falcon, 1942) *was the start of the private eye cycle which flourished balefully through the 1940s. . . . The best of it came from Raymond Chandler who wrote the Philip Marlowe thrillers. . . .'*

Philip Oakes, *The Thriller*, Cinema Part 5, *The Sunday Times*

1. A selection of films based upon the books of the authors in this anthology. Titles in brackets are those given by the film studios.

CHANDLER, Raymond

Farewell My Lovely. R. K. O. Radio Pictures Ltd, 1942. (The Falcon Takes Over.)

Farewell My Lovely. R. K. O. Radio Pictures Ltd, 1944.

The Big Sleep. Warner Brothers Pictures Ltd, 1946.

The Lady in the Lake. Metro-Goldwyn-Mayer Ltd, 1946.

The High Window. Twentieth Century Fox Ltd, 1947. (The Brasher Doubloon.)

The Little Sister. Metro-Goldwyn-Mayer Ltd, 1969. (Marlow.)

ELLIN, Stanley

Dreadful Summit. United Artists' Corporation, 1954. (The Big Night.)

FAULKNER, William

Sanctuary. Paramount Productions Ltd, 1933. (The Story of Temple Drake.)

Intruder in the Dust. Metro-Goldwyn-Mayer Ltd, 1949.

Requiem for a Nun. Twentieth Century Fox Ltd, 1960. (Sanctuary.)

Sanctuary. Twentieth Century Fox Ltd, 1960.

FITZGERALD, F. Scott
The Great Gatsby. Paramount Productions Ltd, 1949.

HAMMETT, Dashiell
The Maltese Falcon. Warner Brothers Pictures Ltd, 1931.
The Thin Man. Metro-Goldwyn-Mayer Ltd, 1934.
The Glass Key. Paramount Productions Ltd, 1935.
The Maltese Falcon (John Huston, dir.). Warner Brothers Pictures Ltd, 1942.
The Glass Key. Paramount Productions Ltd, 1942.

HEMINGWAY, Ernest
To Have and Have Not. Warner Brothers Pictures Ltd, 1944.
The Killers. Universal Motion Pictures Ltd, 1946.
The Killers. Rank Film Distributors, 1964.

MILLER, Arthur
Death of a Salesman. Columbia Pictures Ltd, 1951.

RUNYON, Damon
Johnny One-Eye. United Artists, 1950.
The Lemon Drop Kid. Paramount Productions Ltd, 1951.
Bloodhounds of Broadway. Twentieth Century Fox Ltd, 1952.
Money From Home. Paramount Productions Ltd, 1953.

WESTLAKE, Donald E.
Point Blank (as Richard Stark). Metro-Goldwyn-Mayer Ltd, 1967.
The Split (as Richard Stark). Metro-Goldwyn-Mayer Ltd, 1968.
The Busy Body. Paramount Productions Ltd, 1968.
The Hot Rock. (How to Steal a Diamond in Six Easy Lessons.) 1972.

2. A selection of films within or closely connected with the genre.

Little Caesar. International Motion Pictures, 1930. Based on a book of the same title by W. R. Burnett.
High Sierra. Warner Brothers Pictures Ltd, 1941. Based on a book of the same title by W. R. Burnett. John Huston assisted on the script.
This Gun for Hire. Paramount Productions Ltd, 1942. W. R. Burnett scripted this from a Graham Greene 'entertainment'.

Double Indemnity. Paramount Productions Ltd, 1944. Based on a story of the same name by James M. Cain. Raymond Chandler worked on the screenplay with Billy Wilder.

The Blue Dahlia. Paramount Productions Ltd, 1946. Original Screenplay by Raymond Chandler. '*The picture is entertaining in a dry, nervous, electric way. It is as neatly stylized and synchronized and as uninterested in moral excitement as a good ballet; it knows its own weight and size perfectly and carries them gracefully and without self-importance; it is, barring occasional victories and noble accidents, about as good a movie as can be expected from the big factories. In its own uninsistent way, for that matter, it does carry a certain amount of social criticism.*' James Agee.

Key Largo. Warner Brothers Pictures Ltd, 1948. Directed by John Huston.

The Asphalt Jungle. Metro-Goldwyn-Mayer Ltd, 1950. Based on a book of the same name by W. R. Burnett, who wrote the screenplay with John Huston, the director.

Murder, Inc. Warner Brothers Pictures Ltd, 1952. Film based on the revelations of Abe Reles about organized crime.

The Big Heat. Columbia Pictures Ltd, 1953. '*. . . the blurring of distinctions between criminality and legality, good and evil, right and wrong.*' Colin McArthur.

On the Waterfront. Columbia Pictures Ltd, 1954. Directed by Elia Kazan.

The Killers. Universal Motion Pictures Ltd, 1964. Far removed from the original Hemingway story but a fine example of the work of Don Siegel.

Harper. Warner Brothers Pictures Ltd, 1966. Based on a book by Ross Macdonald, *The Moving Target*. An attempt to recreate the private eye mood of the forties.

Bonnie and Clyde. Warner Brothers Pictures Ltd, 1967. Directed by Arthur Penn. '*. . . to be admired on a dozen or so levels—as a great piece of myth-making, as a haunting evocation of time just past, as a social document, as a harrowing psychological study, as a jaunty legend which becomes tragedy without once breaking its stride.*' Philip Oakes.

Bullitt. Warner Brothers Pictures Ltd, 1968. Produced by Peter Yates, an English director.

Gumshoe. Memorial Pictures Ltd, 1972. Neville Smith's nostalgic recreation of the clichés of the genre.

3. A selection of film extracts or complete films available in 16 mm for hire by schools. They are arranged according to source of hire.

The British Film Institute, 81 Dean Street, London, W.1.
Complete Films
Little Caesar. 1930. 80 mins.
Murder, Inc. 1951. 84 mins.

Film Study Extracts
The Big Heat. 1953. 13 mins.
Little Caesar. 1930. 11 mins.
The Maltese Falcon. 1942. 9 mins.
Baby Face Nelson. 1957. 8 mins.

Columbia Pictures (16 mm), Film House, 142 Wardour Street, London, W.1.
The Glass Key. 1942. 85 mins.
This Gun For Hire. 1942. 81 mins.
Double Indemnity. 1944. 107 mins.
The Blue Dahlia. 1945. 99 mins.
The Big Heat. 1953. 89 mins.
On the Waterfront. 1954. 107 mins.
The Killers. 1964. 94 mins.
Gumshoe. 1971. 84 mins.

Film Distributors Associated (16 mm) Ltd, P.O. Box 2JL, Mortimer House, 37/41 Mortimer Street, London, W.1.
Little Caesar. 1930. 80 mins.
High Sierra. 1941. 100 mins.
The Maltese Falcon. 1941. 100 mins.

Robert Kingston Films Ltd, 645/7 Uxbridge Road, Hayes End, Middlesex.
Farewell My Lovely. 1945. 85 mins.
Crossfire. 1947. 86 mins.

Rank Film Library, P.O. Box 70, Great West Road, Brentford, Middlesex.
Harper (*The Moving Target*). 1966. 121 mins.
Bonnie and Clyde. 1967. 111 mins.
Point Blank. 1967. 92 mins.
Bullitt. 1968. 114 mins.
Klute. 1971. 114 mins.

Ron Harris Cinema Services Ltd, Glenbuck House, Glenbuck Road, Surbiton, Surrey.
Lady in the Lake. 1946. 103 mins.
Intruder in the Dust. 1950. 86 mins.
The Asphalt Jungle 1950. 105 mins.
Marlowe (The Little Sister). 1969. 95 mins.

Acknowledgments

The Publisher acknowledges with thanks permissions granted by the following for the use of copyright material:

Hamish Hamilton Ltd for 'I'll Be Waiting' from *The Smell of Fear* by Raymond Chandler, © 1965 Helga Greene; Curtis Brown Ltd for 'The Day of the Bullet' from Stanley Ellin's *The Blessington Method*; Chatto & Windus Ltd for 'The Liar' from William Faulkner's *New Orleans Sketches*; Harold Matson Company Inc. for Dashiell Hammett's 'The Gatewood Caper' from *The Big Knockover*, © 1962 by Lillian Hellman; Jonathan Cape Ltd and the Executors of the Ernest Hemingway Estate for Chapter 10 from *To Have and Have Not*; Elaine Greene Ltd for Arthur Miller's 'It Takes a Thief', © 1947 by Arthur Miller; Constable & Co. Ltd, for 'The Snatching of Bookie Bob' from Damon Runyon's *Runyon on Broadway;* Henry Morrison Inc., N.Y. for Donald E. Westlake's 'Best Friend Murder'; Joe Gores for his story 'Goodbye, Pops' and Laurence Pollinger for F. Scott Fitzgerald's 'Mystery of the Raymond Mortgage'.

The photograph on the cover is reproduced by permission of Warner Brothers Pictures Ltd. It is a still from *The Big Sleep* (1946).